D1266942

ANATOMY OF CENSORSHIP

Why the Censors Have it Wrong

Harry White

University Press of America, Inc.
Lanham • New York • Oxford

Copyright © 1997 by
University Press of America,® Inc.
4720 Boston Way
Lanham, Maryland 20706

12 Hid's Copse Rd.
Cummor Hill, Oxford OX2 9JJ

Library of Congress Cataloging-in-Publication Data

White, Harry..
Anatomy of censorship : why the censors have it wrong / Harry White.
p. cm.
Includes bibliographical references.
l. Censorship--United States. I. Title.
Z658.U5W49   1997 363.3'l--dc21 97-29620 CIP
12 2

ISBN 0-7618-0701-2 (cloth: alk. ppr.)

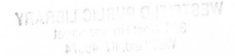 ™ The paper used in this publication meets the minimum
requirements of American National Standard for information
Sciences—Permanence of Paper for Printed Library Materials,
ANSI Z39.48—1984

Contents

Preface

Censorship, whether it has to do with legal judgments or simply a warning about what not to say at the company picnic, usually involves the subjects of religion, sex and politics. Some background information might give the reader some idea of my personal involvement in these concerns.

My first encounter with the problem of free speech might be said to have occurred when I was about five years of age: One of my playmates called me a dirty Jew. This I could not comprehend. "Why," I asked my mother, "does Junior call me dirty when he is never clean?"

At eleven I understood better. By then my family had moved to an apartment across the street from a church. The boys who hung out round the church would see me leave my building, follow me a few blocks from the church, and call me a dirty Jew. No change there. But then they would proceed to beat me up. And thus did I develop a vivid understanding of the problem. What I learned was that first of all, anyone who called me a dirty Jew was a damned fool. Secondly I learned that what really hurt was my bloody lip and skull, and so far as I was concerned, they could, if they wished, call me whatever they wanted so long as they stopped beating me up. As I would learn even later, Thomas Jefferson put it quite well some time ago. Speech, he said, neither picks my pocket nor breaks my leg. And I just didn't want my bones broken.

This experience prepared me for, among other things, the era of hate speech codes in which I now teach. Someone like myself who has been called a dirty Jew does not have much sympathy with hate speech codes because being called a dirty Jew taught me how much better a person I was than the people who hang around street corners waiting to beat up Jews. And although I recognize the greater disadvantages which women and minorities face in today's world, I cannot believe that all these so-called victims of hate speech posses fewer resources or intelligence or simple moxie than an eleven-year old child so that their lives will fall into ruin because of the words some fool utters. The real issues our society has failed to adequately address are not racism or sexism, but racial and sexual discrimination, and the emphasis upon racist or sexist thought and expression not only smacks of totalitarianism in the kinds of controls it would institute, but it has diverted many of us from these substantive issues. People's lives are ruined by their inability (often due to racial, gender, and sexual discrimination) to earn a decent living, have a secure job and a place to live, receive adequate health and retirement benefits and so on. My guess is that once people have these things they will pretty much be able to find the friends and acquaintances who like and respect them and will less likely give a damn what others might think or say.

As I grew up, I received what in late twentieth-century America was a typical Jewish upbringing. My paternal grandmother who lived with us the first seven years of my life was an orthodox Jew. My maternal grandfather had been a Eugene Debs socialist who would feed me bacon, lettuce and tomato sandwiches to put some balance back in his grandson's life. I also received a typical Hebrew education which meant going to Hebrew classes four days a week after school let out, and at thirteen I was bar mitzvahed which meant that now I could play baseball after school let out any day of the week when it didn't rain, or football when it didn't snow too hard.

My children also received a typical Hebrew education, and when my older son (I have two) was about to be bar mitzvahed I returned for the first time in years to a synagogue. My first impression was that the sense of community was perhaps nice after all. But then the rabbi got up to speak, and it wasn't that I did not agree with what he said (it had to do with Israeli policy). It was that as I looked around the room every man and woman *without exception* was nodding in agreement! Then I remembered: that's why I left! I had found many things disagreeable, and the promise and the expectation was that if anyone wanted to be part of this comforting life he or she was not supposed to disagree.

Disagreeable people like me find themselves holding opinions which many others find uncomfortable, offensive or threatening (we haven't yet learned to talk only about the weather when invited to parties or company picnics). We campaign or vote for more losers than the average citizen. We find ourselves constantly in the 5% column when Gallup or Harris poles come out, and we worry that if we ever wind up in the 65% column it might indicate not that America is finally moving in the right political direction, but that we have simply grown soft with age. We worry also when we hear politicians say that "the American people" don't want this or that because we have never quite felt that these politicians have us in mind when they intone the words *American* and *people*. And they are no doubt right, for their itemized list of what Americans don't want very often contains exactly the things we want for America. And when scholars, politicians, and moral and religious leaders talk about virtue and morality we get really frightened. We know it isn't going to be the Buddhists in San Francisco or the *Hasidim* in Brooklyn, our gay neighbors, the head of the woman's study program or any of the friends one acknowledges in a book who will determine for the American people what virtue is. We know who they will be. They will, as always, be Christian, they will be white, they will be male, have more power and money than most of the rest of us, and the rest of us will have to retire to the closet of silence so as not to offend our acquaintances and co-workers, in order to protect our jobs and not get our lips bloodied again. When politicians and other public figures start talking about virtue we also recognize that they aren't talking about leading good and decent lives, but about conformity to the opinions, beliefs and values they and theirs hold and which they would like to see enforced throughout the land.

And in modern bourgeois society the opinions one must be most silent about usually have to do with matters of sex. Thus one can read dozens of articles and books on the subject of pornography and find writers and scholars ridiculing the prudishness of the censor, defending free expression, the rights of others to read what they want, but, with rare exceptions, no one defends pornography itself or *his* right to read it. (The rare exceptions these days are usually women, more frequently outspoken lesbians, and that is perhaps because of the way the politically correct winds have shifted: a sexual male is today often regarded as a sexist pig and a potential rapist whereas as a sexual female represents a liberated woman. It would be difficult to find any man or even woman writing about the subject with the honesty and insight of someone like Susie Bright--a breath of fresh air where stuffiness tends to characterize all sides on the issue.) One for instance finds in one's readings statements like that of a leading liberal thinker who in criticizing attempts to censor pornography feels he must note that of course liberals find pornography disgusting, as if liberals are constituted differently from other mortals and for them viewing pictures of beautiful, naked men and women makes them want to retch.

More commonly one encounters book length studies on the history of the subject which will say something like, In the course of my research I have managed to collect most of the work of Betty Page. Or, I have had--during the course of my research--occasion in my travels to visit sex clubs in Scandinavia, or S and M shows in New York. Then there are those studies on the aesthetics of pornography which appear as inappropriate in their analysis as all those outrageous explanations from psychologists and feminists as to the real reasons why men indulge in it. There are indeed some sound, sensible and insightful studies of pornography. (In addition to some listed in my bibliography I should note F. M. Christensen's *Pornography: The Other Side* which is perhaps the best extended essay on the subject.) But in the end pornography is justified because people feel it needs to be justified and they wind up making incredible claims for it when I suppose the answer is simple. There are variations, to be sure, but it no doubt goes something like this: When it comes to pornography the persons on the pages look a heck of a lot better than either you or anyone you've dated, these incredibly gorgeous women will not reject you or require a lot of time and money, you won't have to lie to them, they won't phone you the next night while you are in the middle of a good book to ask what you've been doing and why you haven't called, and when you are reading Virginia Woolf, Betty Page will not run out of the closet to ask with angry tears in her eyes, "Who is that woman and why are you ignoring me?"

That one of pornography's leading advantages is that it circumvents all the complexities and difficulties of sexual relations means in the end that it does not serve, as many contend, as a substitute for sexual relations. Viewing pornography may divert one for a time from the knowledge that he has no sexual relationships, or that his job is also not going well, or that all men are mortal and he is but a man with a persistent pain in his side; but if one wants conversation, companionship, love and affection one knows very well that these things will not be found within the adult section of the local video store, where even eye contact, let alone conversation ("Seen any good movies lately?"), is shunned. If love and affection could be gotten at the video counter, the tapes would rent for more than three dollars a night, but then the clerk might refuse to rent them to you for the reason that he hardly knows you and you didn't ask nice.

True, we must be objective or at least present an air of objectivity in our studies, but defending the right to free expression while hiding behind our footnotes is not exactly the most openly courageous stand one might take. I can't really blame those who treat the subject in that way. The pressures are enormous, the consequences might prove difficult (to say the least), but give me a break. People usually tend to write about what they are interested in. Religion and politics have interested me and I've written and published about the subjects (to the amazement of many, I'm sure, my other publications will not be listed anywhere in the book). And I also find the sight of beautiful women interesting and stimulating and pleasurable. It can't compare with *Pride and Prejudice*, but then again, when it comes to sheer, raw excitement, *Pride and Prejudice* can't really compare with *Debbie Does Dallas*. (The shower scene alone provides a wonderful illustration of what can happen when things go wrong and there's not enough money in the budget to re-shoot the scene. *Cinema verite* at its best!).

What can I say? I can't understand it. There must be something wrong with me--at least wise men and of late women who would claim to be wise have been writing and telling me so. Now there is a lot wrong with me, but the opinions I hold regarding religion or politics or sex, and the desires I have are not among the problems I need to worry myself about. It has taken me some time to figure that out, so that those things I believe and enjoy are not a problem for me, however much others have claimed to be troubled or offended by them. And having taught for about three decades, I have found that perhaps most of my students do not agree with the opinions I express in class, but over the years I have noted the regular few who sit silently in the back of the room and take heart that a university professor is telling them what they've so often thought and didn't dare express. And over the years not a few have come to thank me for my irreverence.

So when one comes to write a book on censorship one hopes of course to inform, enlighten, and perhaps persuade. But the issues cut so deeply to the core of what people feel are so important to their lives that one suspects he will merely be left preaching to the converted or those just waiting to be converted. But that could be an achievement in itself. As I have been encouraged by the men and women who have written insightfully on these subjects, I would hope to encourage those who think and feel differently from most others in these matters. Readers might perhaps recognize that they are not in the wrong after all, and when measuring themselves in the gloom of the traditional and conventional wisdom of the day, it is not a case of "all good to me is lost; evil, be thou my good." For the real evil in the world comes not from the disagreeable people, but from those so convinced of the absolute rightness of their opinions and beliefs that they would impose what they think and feel on others. It is they who must account for their actions. For it is they who are most definitely in the wrong and from whom little good ever comes

At the very least, if one still feels he or she is stuck with some really goofy notions, take heart, my friend, you aren't the only oddball out there.

Acknowledgments

Someone has written (though I forgot to write it down myself) that the reasons given for censorship are stupid. So a book like this one must first acknowledge those who have called for and enforced censorship-- acknowledge them because they tend to do it with reasoning that is so often so illogical, ill-founded, intolerant, inhumane, mean-spirited and wrongheaded that the task of discrediting them becomes a relatively easy one. When comparing their words with what I write on the subject, some readers might get the impression that I am smarter than I actually am, though fairness dictates that I also acknowledge that many will find my own reasoning equally ill advised (more about that shortly).

Acknowledgments usually end by thanking one's wife for her patience and understanding or someone identified only by initials (who--one can only guess--may be the Dean's wife or, these days, a same sex life partner). If the writer was born a German national somewhere between let's say 1893 and 1913, he will be sure to point out that he left the country in 1933, and just about everyone will finally note that the opinions expressed are strictly one's own. Let me however begin by saying that I don't have a wife, have no interest in D. R. or L. T. (in fact I don't believe I've ever met them), I am not German born, though the German nation about the time I was born in the United States made sure some of my ancestors never got to go anywhere ever again, and lastly the thoughts I express are anything but my own. They are largely the result of that wonderful alchemy of reading and reflection, in this case an insignificant offshoot of the thinking of men like Chuang-tzu, William Blake, Frederich Nietzsche, Walter Kaufmann, Karl Popper, and Isaiah Berlin. What these men in particular have helped me understand is that stunning intelligence comes not from intellectual brilliance, but from intellectual honesty: the honesty and courage, which too few intellectuals posses, to proclaim simple, plain truths which everyone somehow already knows to be true, but which they have not yet brought themselves to think or dared to say--and to proclaim them in the face of various groups and institutions established to uphold traditional and conventional wisdom. That to me is the mark of true genius.

I am also not alone in my thinking because of the companionship, while I did my research and writing, of some especially fine friends--Ellen Domke, Gene Kukso, Rick Rozoff, Leo Segedin, and Bill Wycislo, who have listened, discussed, argued, suggested further reading before I dare to speak to them again, or who have no doubt just been bored over a good dinner they had been looking forward to.

I would like also to thank the university that employs me for *not* granting me a sabbatical for this project and forbid them to take any credit for it. There is important research going on at universities throughout the world for which grant money and release time from teaching are needed, but for many of us university professors, teaching is a part time job for which, given our education and expertise, we receive part time pay, and if we weren't interested in reading, researching, writing and teaching, we could be earning really good money. In our situation however there is usually plenty of time to do all we need to do or shouldn't be doing, and I am proud to say that, with a couple of possible exceptions, I have done all my work without receiving grants or release time.

Over the years I have worked with many fine professors, students, and staff who have made teaching a wonderful experience I would not trade for any other profession, but as for the university, I am still in the position where I can say I really owe them nothing special and they don't reward me enough in either recognition or money that I have to do what they tell me. Wonderful thing that academic freedom! It's worth, I figure, an additional $50,000 dollars a year which I could be making if I wanted to earn a respectable living by censoring what I think and feel.

So to Helen Johnson, Tom Pawlek, and Kathy Snyder for assisting me over the last months in preparing my book for publication I owe many thanks. Special thanks to Kimberly Dudash for doing (in the words of my editor) "a wonderful job" of formatting the entire work for publication, and special thanks (and more) as well to Brian White for doing a final, careful proofread of the work.

My thanks then to all those who have listened and spoken to me, in friendship or even at times in the heat of anger, knowing that to be free to speak one's mind is not only a basic liberty one must fight to preserve, but the basis of what makes for fondness and friendship at the deepest levels.

Introduction

Essays on censorship tend to be polemical, often involving special pleadings for or against the suppression of certain material. Longer studies will survey its history, usually concentrating on examples of a particular type, such as the censorship of religious or sexual expression. In both cases, writers focus mostly upon the content of expression, and since what constitutes objectionable or illicit expression in one country or culture will be perfectly acceptable in another, this emphasis upon content does not get us very close to understanding the general nature of censorship itself.

The questions we might ask are: What are the conditions which regularly prompt censorship? Can we discover common concerns which tend to appear over and again in different times and places? Do the rationales for censorship tend to repeat the same or similar justifications? Do these justifications reveal or mask the censor's true concerns?

I think these types of questions regarding censorship should not only be asked, but they can also be answered. And those answers should tell us a lot about the nature and general characteristics of censorship wherever and whenever it tends to occur. What they will help us to recognize is that the censors are usually wrong. This is not to say that they are morally wrong. I do believe that with one possible exception (discussed later) that everyone ought to be able to say and hear or write and read whatever he or she pleases, even if that means offending a lot of other people, and those who are offended should have no right to regulate what others may read or write. However, I do not wish to argue against the censors in that way--although I'm sure I shall not be able to resist it entirely. When I say they are wrong, what I mean to show is that the reasons given by censors for their actions are usually not the reasons why censorship is imposed. Censors are wrong because they do not understand the nature and purpose of censorship, even their own, any better than anybody else. By studying the conditions and stated reasons for censorship we may better understand not only the nature of censorship, but how the rationales often given for it are simply false and inaccurate.

For now, by way of introduction, let me propose the following: Censors regularly claim that they seek to restrict the expression of ideas that might be misleading and false or are dangerous and have a tendency to harm, but this claim runs into two basic difficulties.

The first is that though censors insist there exists certain material which is inherently pernicious, they never seem willing or able to define with any clarity what it is.   No one ever seems to know what   constitutes blasphemous, obscene, or seditious expression.   Clear definitions and standards are rarely publicized prior to the arrest, prosecution and conviction of those accused of illicit expression.

The second major difficulty censors face is that they cannot demonstrate that the material they do suppress actually poses a danger to society. The censor's claim to be acting in society's interest by prohibiting what is harmful or false is usually itself false and inaccurate.   For censors consistently target opinions which they find offensive and which for that reason alone they assume to be false or dangerous as well, but in the final analysis they have to forcibly suppress these opinions precisely because they are unable to convincingly demonstrate that what they contend about them is in fact true. Censorship is most likely to occur not when opinions appear that are indeed shown and therefore known to be harmful.   Just the opposite occurs. Censorship arises when and precisely because someone *cannot* convincingly demonstrate to others that the opinions which offend him or her are indeed truly false or dangerous.   If they could, there would after all be little or no need for censorship.

I have said that I believe that censorship is wrong, but I believe it is wrong because it is unnecessary. Let me make my position clear from the start: A lot will be made in upcoming discussion about facts and values.   To contend, as I do throughout, that moral opinions cannot be demonstrated is not to say that there are no moral tendencies.   I believe that there is ample evidence from biology, ethology, anthropology, as well as ordinary human experience, that we possess moral sensibilities and tendencies built into our nature. Compassion, altruism, caring for children, parents and kin, sharing, and kindness, even often to strangers, are universally valued and practiced within various societies and communities.   There is also a general absence of murder, incest, rape, and theft.   This is so universally true that when the opposite occurs, it amounts to news, and many wrongly conclude from these newsworthy exceptions that murder and mayhem is the way of the world. What unfortunately seems also to be universally true is that the moral behavior which is amply evident within a group does not usually extend--certainly not with the same dependability--beyond it to members of other groups. Thus prejudice, intolerance, hatred, torture, warfare, exploitation, and enslavement have also been universally practiced and even valued with regard to individuals and groups outside one's own community or society.

Censorship characteristically aims at controlling the ideas within a particular group or society and not the ideas of those outside the community: Americans do not censor the citizens of Sweden, nor did the Catholic Index of Prohibited Books seek to control the reading habits of Muslims. If censorship does have anything to do with prejudice and intolerance, it probably serves to foster them, but the practical question is how it serves to affect the behavior of individuals within the community it targets, and here it seems that the ideas censors insist are so important that they need to be protected really do not have that great an effect upon our conduct. It is primarily people who wish to promote the value of some institution or belief system upon which their own status often depends who will argue the importance of beliefs--that, for example, without a belief in the existence of their God or an afterlife everything would be permitted, or that without the attitudes promoted by pornography the treatment of women would significantly improve. This despite the fact that the mistreatment of women was as great or greater before the advent of pornography and that the overwhelming majority of prisoners in any country are believers and people who believe differently or not at all don't on that account appear to behave any worse than anybody else.

Censorship is usually defended as being necessary for the preservation of the moral order upon which each and every citizen or subject depends for his or her safety and well-being and upon which society as a whole depends for its very preservation. However, it is more to the point to say that censorship and its attending legal controls and enforcement serves to protect the predominant ideology from which those benefit most who have attained power, wealth, status, and control within society. These persons seek to protect the prevailing ideology (or ideologies) not because society would, as they contend, otherwise collapse, but because it serves to legitimize their eminence and the various social, political and economic arrangements they oversee. The controlling ideology will of course be particularly effective if the distribution of power, resources, and benefits within society, the relative lower status and obedience of other members and classes is generally accepted as right and true and just and natural or divinely ordained. To question these ideologies could lead to social change, that is, a redistribution of resources and benefits, a re-alignment of political power, and a re-arrangement of social relationships, but it will not lead to moral collapse or the destruction of society, as we so often hear when attempts are made to justify things like censorship.

In his novel, *The Idiot*, Dostoyevsky, a typical critic of modernity, typically has one of his characters tell us that what we lack is "an idea that binds men together today with half the strength as in" medieval times. The "binding idea doesn't exist anymore." It is probably true, as I will argue, that ideas serve as much or more to divide men than to bind them together. The turmoil and bloodshed which sometimes accompanies changes in ideas is not do mostly to the presence of bad ideas or absence of good ones, but to the fact that men who espouse different and often conflicting ideas attach such overrated importance to them that they are foolish and cruel enough to fight and kill for them (a point I address in the last section of this essay). Still and all, the usual turn of events is that when a "binding idea" is challenged, lost or replaced, a few people will likely lose their positions of authority, but societies will not likely come undone. Various leaders and authority figures come and go as the absolutely necessary ideas they preach are found to be not so necessary after all and are replaced by other supposedly equally binding ideas. Yet throughout almost every one of these changes we do not find societies collapsing or people suddenly rushing madly to experience and perpetrate previously unknown evils and crimes. For the fact of the matter is that most all men and women, including intellectuals who dwell on these concerns, have always managed their lives without giving hardly the least thought to the moral and religious issues which a few authority figures, again mostly for their own aggrandizement, insist are crucial to leading a good, healthy, moral life.

This is not to say that ideas have no importance, but that they impact upon the authority of the few more than moral character of the many. The result of not controlling "dangerous" ideas is therefore just the opposite of what the censor contends--that an eminent few are somehow immune to the harmful effects from which they must protect the vulnerable and often unwary majority. For it is the few who are most vulnerable to changes in ideas and whom censorship serves to protect. That is why, as we shall see, censors have an almost impossible time trying to convince people that the expression they would regulate needs to be regulated for the reason that it is inherently immoral or potentially dangerous to society at large. As we shall see censorship tends to be initiated not, as some would have us think, in response to the emergence of evil ideas that might lead to corruption and depravity, but in response to the advent of new media of communication which threaten exclusive rule by making ideas that have often been around for quite a long time available to classes of people who did not formerly have access to them. Moral decency, the good society does not rise or fall on the moral, religious or political ideas our leaders and authority figures insist must be maintained, even through the force of law when necessary. Within any society, people can be expected to lead moral lives or, with a few regular exceptions, immoral lives, regardless of the beliefs and opinions those in high positions insist need protecting.

There are certainly real problems every society faces and needs to confront--economic, legal, political, moral. What people think or believe is not one of them. What they say, write, paint, film, or photograph and what they hear, see, or read, if it is a problem at all, remains a long way down the list of serious concerns any society needs to confront. This is not to say that government ought not to interfere in these areas, but that the safety and well-being of individuals in society and that of society as a whole will not be adversely affected if government refrains from interfering. Indeed, for the most part, society will not be well served from such interference and will more likely be materially harmed in ways much more evident than by the so-called harms said to be caused by various types of expression.

What moral, religious, and political leaders and authorities can be credited with when they enforce censorship is not the preservation or improvement of moral conduct, but the invention of special moral categories. Censorship operates on the assumption that the thoughts, feelings, opinions, beliefs and fantasies of human beings ought to be a subject of moral judgment and ultimately social and government action. These should never be the subject of moral scrutiny any more than a preference for Monet over Picasso or broccoli over carrots should be a matter of grave social interest and moral scrutiny. Such a view, I believe, is neither amoral nor tolerant to the point of nihilism and anarchy as some charge. It represents a strong, highly practical moral position which holds that it is incredibly wasteful and unnecessarily cruel to punish people for their thoughts and opinions. Were government to get out of the business of censorship and re-allocate the funds regularly spent on it, such a move would lead to an unburdening of the legal system (both the legislative and judicial branches) and a re-deployment of federal, state, and local law enforcement agents so as to better confront the real dangers and serious crimes citizens face. It is also neither a cynical nor a naively optimistic view, but a position which believes that under normal conditions (which are after all the norm) human beings will generally behave morally towards others, regardless of what they might think or feel. And if they do not, as a few regularly do not, the reasons almost never have to do with the belief systems censorship seeks to enforce.

Chapter 1

The Problem of Definition

Judgments as to what constitutes illicit expression vary over time and among jurisdictions, and not infrequently the same material may at one and the same time and place be censored in one form (comic books and cinema) and unregulated in another (novels and plays), so it is next to, if not completely impossible to determine on the basis of content alone what constitutes objectional material. Yet those who believe there is or ought to be such a thing as illicit expression think they can find a set of characteristics within the works themselves which makes them by their very nature immoral, indecent, and offensive. These persistent attempts to formulate general, content based definitions of obscenity or blasphemy remain doomed from the start in large part because they involve what philosophers call a category mistake.

We do not ordinarily mistake literary or artistic terms, such as *sonnet* or *still life*, for legal terms, but we do repeatedly mistake legal terms such as *profanity* or *obscenity* for literary or artistic definitions and regularly think that by identifying a work as obscene we are actually describing some characteristic that is discoverable within the work itself, comparable to identifying a sonnet as a fourteen line poem or a painting of a bowl of fruit as a still life.

Profanity and *obscenity*, like *felon* or *convict*, are legal terms, and as such they do not describe inherent characteristics, but merely status under the law. To say that a man is funny, ill-tempered, or shy describes characteristics of the man, however to say that a man is a murderer, that according to the law he has been found guilty of murder, describes nothing of the man's character. By the same token, to say that a painting depicts a naked couple or an essay deals with the subject of atheism describes the works, but to identify those same works as obscene or blasphemous merely indicates their status under the law of a particular jurisdiction and not the nature of their content. That is perhaps the major reason why, as Bernard Arcand noted, "The first mistake made by many theorists attempting to define pornography has been their assumption that it is possible to pinpoint a particular and identifiable content" (27, that mistake is of course not limited to terms like *pornography*). Thus if said theorist were to place an underground copy of James Joyce's *Ulysses* next to a copy of the Random House publication of James Joyce's *Ulysses* which appeared after Judge Woolsey declared the work not to be obscene, he would discover that the illicit, obscene version is identical in content to the legal publication, just as *Memoirs of a Woman of Pleasure* (a.k.a. *Fanny Hill*), which remained unregulated during the life of its author, John Cleland, has not one word different from, is exactly the same as the "pornographic" novel which would be censored for over a hundred years after Cleland's death.

Dictionary definitions don't do much either to help us discover what in the work itself makes it obscene. *Obscene*, according to the *Random House College Dictionary*, means: "1. Offensive to modesty or decency; indecent, lewd. 2. Causing or intended to cause sexual excitement or lust. 3. Abominable or disgusting; repulsive." In every instance the dictionary defines *obscene* not by identifying any essential quality within the work or expression, but by describing effects and responses. Moreover the defining effects and responses are not merely inconsistent, but they can even be diametrically opposed: A work that is obscene may at one and the same time evoke sexual excitement and lust in some and disgust and revulsion in others.

So it would appear that one reason we cannot arrive at a consistent definition or a universal standard of obscenity is that the term does not define an objective characteristic of a work but various subjective responses to it. Well, not quite. The dictionary definitions present us with yet another category mistake. For it may be that our actual responses to obscene material are not actually that divergent, and therefore what the dictionary identifies as responses really amount to something other or more than just responses.

In other areas, subjective responses are not usually all that different. By way of comparison take for example our experience of color. Even though we have been told that black is not a color but the absence of color and that white is the reflection of all colors of the spectrum, we do not experience them that way, nor do we perceive blue as a particular wavelength on the electro-magnetic spectrum and red as a somewhat longer wavelength. But even though it may therefore be true that black and white and red and blue aren't really "out there" in the objective world just as obscenity is not actually in the work, it is nevertheless true and we know it as a matter of fact that dirt is black, milk white, apples red and the sky blue. These are indeed objective facts about the real world we all know and experience because whatever may "really and truly be out there" independent of our experience, we all experience milk as white and so on. In other words we can establish inter-subjective agreement: two or more people observing a glass of milk from different viewpoints, or even at different times and places, will all report it to be white. So we can state as a true fact of the world we all share in common that milk is white, which means also that the statements "milk is white" or "milk is black" are verifiable. They can be shown to be either true or false (more about this shortly).

The same cannot be said of statements regarding the nature of things like obscenity. They do not, as it were, behave in the same way. Thus the fact that definitions of obscenity tend to vary and are often irreconcilable does not indicate that we are after all simply dealing with subjective responses, as the dictionary definitions, for one, would seem to suggest. For the subjective responses of various persons can after all often be quite consistent. What we are dealing with here are reactions that are inconsistent and irreconcilable because they characteristically change when standpoints change. If they are responses, they are significantly different in that they are responses which we cannot count on being the same for any two people, cannot count on them being responses that define a world shared in common. All of this means, finally, that we are dealing with something which is certainly subjective but about which we can establish no inter-subjective agreement. Something which behaves the way it does because it falls into the category not of facts nor responses, but of opinions.

That milk is white is a fact, that *Memoirs of a Woman of Pleasure* can stimulate responses like sexual excitement in (some of) its readers is also a fact, but that the book is obscene is an opinion, and one cannot say *as a matter of fact* that it or any other work is or is not obscene. The reason all these dictionary and, as we shall see, legal definitions vary is because they are describing not facts, or even general responses, but opinions, and they do indeed describe them very well, because it is in the very nature of opinions to remain various and inconsistent regardless of what the subject matter may be. Opinions, unlike facts and many human responses, make up worlds of experience which we decidedly do not share in common and cannot establish any agreement on.

Opponents of censorship will often note that the censor claims to know what obscenity or profanity is, yet he cannot define it. But even opponents of censorship cannot (so far as I can tell) explain exactly why it is impossible to offer general definitions of these terms. No general definition of illicit expression is possible because in most every instance censorship is based upon and seeks to regulate opinion, and characteristically in matters of opinion, no general agreement can ever possibly be achieved. (This point is, I believe, so essential to understanding the reasons for censorship that I shall return to it as the subject of our last chapter.)

So we should not be misled, first of all, into thinking that definitions of obscenity can, or do indeed, or were ever intended to define some universal, objective quality inherent in expression, any more than *pain* describes a quality within the knife upon which you cut your hand. Moreover, while it is true that *pain* does not describe a quality in the knife that cuts you, that is not the same as saying that *obscenity* does not describe a quality within a work. Everyone responds with pain when they cut themselves, we may speak of it as a universal response, but not everyone experiences the same work as obscene because even though definitions of obscenity, as we have seen, often purport to be dealing with and describing responses, *obscene* does not describe a response so much as an opinion. They describe opinions as if they were responses and involve us in yet another category mistake.

Works of art or literature can and do produce physiological responses in us. We laugh, we cry, we become sexually aroused. But we also often offer our opinion of a work in terms of a response which never really occurs and which we do not really experience. When I say "Bach moves me to tears" I may very well be describing how I actually respond to the music of Bach, but when I say "Franz Lizst's music stinks" I do not mean and no one takes me to mean that I respond to the *Dante Symphony* or *Mephisto Waltz* by curling my lips and covering my nose to stop myself from gagging. The famous nineteenth-century music critic Eduard Hanslick said of Tchaikovsky's violin concerto that it was music that "stinks in the ear." A wonderful synaesthetic slur, and we appreciate it as such, but we often need to be reminded that music doesn't stink in the nose either. (If it did then the deaf could serve as our best music critics and, like canaries in coal mines, could give us early warning of just where the foul music was coming from.)

Generally our responses to what we call stinking or disgusting works are really no different from the ways we respond to any other work: they don't stink in the nose or disturb our stomachs. However, when we speak of obscene works as disgusting (as is the case in various definitions of them) we really do take seriously the idea that they actually can and do disgust us when in fact they most likely do not.

People may truly respond with lust or indifference to an obscene work, but not usually with disgust and revulsion. Of course one can certainly understand how some people may honestly and truly be disgusted by pornography, that they really and truly respond by wincing, looking away, or even getting sick to their stomachs. Perhaps they might be exposed to a pornographic film depicting couples turned on by coprophagy or have in their hands a copy of *Ulysses* which Judge Woolsey declared not to be obscene for the reason that he found the sex in it to be "emetic, not aphrodisiac" (apparently he thought it better for the health and well-being of American society to have a book circulating that made people vomit rather than one that made them lustful). However, one can also understand that most ordinary, healthy individuals of both sexes, if exposed to pornography depicting that which falls within a certain range of so-called normal sexual experience will in fact most likely respond to it in the same or similar ways: they will respond with interest and pleasure. Some may respond with indifference, but very, very few will respond with actual disgust. So if we are truly talking about responses we may expect that most humans, who have been fruitful and multiplying by means of sexual reproduction since the days of *Genesis*, will have a generally positive response to sexual material. If obscenity definitions were truly based solely upon responses, one might expect considerable agreement among them, since it is fair to assume that the actual responses themselves which most people have to pornographic, or if one wishes, erotic depictions of attractive men and women is probably the same or similar, in the way that being cut by a knife or refreshed by a cool drink is similar for most all people. But one reason we do not find general agreement is that the definitions claim to be describing responses but are actually dealing with something else, not the response sexual beings have to sexual material, but their opinions regarding such material and the usual effects it has on people.

So it is entirely possible that while most all people will respond in somewhat similar ways to sexual material, many of them, including many of those who do indeed respond positively, will nevertheless be *of the opinion* that the material and their response to it is "disgusting." That is the important thing. Major censorship rulings (cited below) purport to control certain responses they claim obscene works elicit--titillation, lust, depravity-- but what they are really after is our opinions regarding these responses rather than the responses themselves. Ultimately it is our opinions respecting our and other people's responses and not the responses themselves that the censor is concerned with and seeks to control. One may not actually find pornography disgusting, but it is important that he or she expresses or endorses the opinion that it is. So *disgust* or *revulsion* in this case do not identify responses, but stated opinions: "Pornography. Disgusting stuff! Me, I never look at it. Threw it in the garbage where it belongs. How can people be turned on by that? I find it disgusting . . . Well, of course, I've never actually thrown up, but it's disgusting nevertheless. Don't give me a hard time. You know what I mean."

Similarly one may read a work blaspheming God or ridiculing Stalin, and that person may actually believe it to be true in what it says, but so long as one holds to the right opinion in his public behavior that is what really counts, at least in the short run. It is perhaps more the job of propaganda to inculcate and influence belief. Censorship may try, and to a great extent it may succeed in controlling belief as well, but that is usually a difficult if not impossible task, to make someone believe what he or she does not or cannot possibly find convincing. Belief is not really a matter of willpower after all. People cannot choose what they believe, but they can choose to give expression to opinions or keep them to themselves. So censorship's real focus has to do not with belief, but with orthodoxy, which literally means straight or correct opinion, and people, especially under conditions of oppression, can readily learn, can be forced to give expression to the correct opinions, regardless of what they really and truly believe. People can be wonderful liars and hypocrites, particularly if it works to their advantage and if they know, for instance, that they will be punished for expressing what those in authority have pronounced to be evil and vicious lies.

Those commonplace definitions which speak of things like obscenity in terms of responses are therefore wrong on two basic counts: The first is that the responses they claim do occur (disgust, depravity, corruption, hatred of and a desire to harm women) rarely if ever do occur (a point to be noted in upcoming discussion). Secondly they are wrong for the reason that even if they do occur, the real issue for society is not fundamentally how people respond to, for example, pornography. The real issue is their opinions regarding those responses. It might therefore be more correct or accurate to say that *obscenity* or *pornography* are terms dealing with the opinions people hold with respect to the responses such works are presumed to elicit. Once we understand the fundamental nature of things like obscenity, that they fall into the category of opinions, and describe neither inherent characteristics nor characteristic responses, we will not be surprised by the fact that we find no general agreement, but often violent disagreement. Nor should we try to resolve the characteristically confusing mess of obscenity definitions nor be confused by them. They do in fact clarify the issue for us by identifying the category of human experience we are dealing with when talking about obscenity and do define what is characteristic about it as well. We are dealing with matters of opinion; and irreconcilability, disagreement, and conflict are what we are familiar with when it comes to matters of opinion. In this respect it is the censor who is confused because he steadfastly refuses to recognize the confusion surrounding the definitions of illicit expression for what it reveals--the variable and conflicting nature of opinion itself--and insists on mistaking differing opinions for something else. Thus we are also quite familiar with those who hold so strongly to their opinions that they often mistake them for general truths or healthy responses next to which the differing opinions of others are therefore held to be falsehoods or symptoms of depravity.

In the final analysis, to ask what in the nature of a work itself constitutes obscenity misses the point because it looks in the wrong direction. Given that the commonplace definitions of obscenity focus upon the responses a work is presumed to elicit in people, responses which are assumed to be characteristically varied and contrary, the practical question has always been not *what* defines obscenity, but *who* defines it. The question has always come down to who, based on his or her personal opinion or beliefs, judges whether something is obscene or not. Insofar as terms like *obscenity* and *pornography* are defined not by identifiable characteristics discoverable within the work, but by peoples' supposed responses to it, *obscenity* and *pornography* are terms that ultimately serve to define people more than expression. As we shall see in the next section, what the censor ultimately seeks to discover and control are not works that are typically obscene, but people who, it is believed, are typically corrupted by works of literature.

Of course the problem of inconsistency we have been examining when it comes to terms like *obscenity* or *blasphemy* is certainly not resolved by turning to legal definitions. In fact there is a serious question whether as legal definitions these terms are in any way meaningful to judges, juries or ordinary citizens.

Additional confusion arises immediately in the area of law. The difficulty is compounded by the fact that *obscenity* or *blasphemy* supposedly serve to define illicit expression, but to rule that obscene or blasphemous expression shall be prohibited merely involves us in an empty tautology which states nothing more than that one should not give expression to what is illegal expression. That is precisely what Lord Kenyon, the Chief Justice of the King's Bench, said when he defined the limits of a free press in England: "The liberty of the press is this, that a man may publish anything which twelve of his countrymen think is not blameable, but that he ought to be punished if he publishes that which is blameable" (*Rex v. Cuthill*, 1799).

Similarly, Lord Devlin, who served on the Queen's Bench from 1948 to 1960, observed that with respect to the legal enforcement of morals, "morality in England means what twelve men and women think it means" (100).

To try and figure from such remarks, put forth by judges who rule on such matters, just what is or is not permissible expression, is next to impossible. And this has remained a persistent problem of modern censorship law--that it characteristically does not present clear notice, prior to publication, of what constitutes illicit expression. This problem of vagueness has arisen in large part because of advances in English law which eliminated the practice of prior restraints upon written material. Under modern Anglo-American law, judgments respecting the legality of expression can be rendered only *after* the fact of publication. That is what Milton argued for in his *Areopagetica,* the elimination of pre-publication restraints, and it is the point of Lord Kenyon's remarks, that liberty of the press means only the absence of prior restraints. In 1906 Justice Holmes made the same observation respecting American law: the constitutional protections declaring freedom of the press, he noted, proposed "to prevent all . . . *previous restraints* upon publications" but did "not prevent the subsequent punishment of such as may be deemed contrary to the public welfare" (qtd. in Nelson 47).

The elimination of prior restraints, the practice of having illicit expression be determined by twelve people only after someone has committed his or her thoughts to publication has meant that prior notice of what constitutes a threat to the public welfare has been hard to come by in modern times. As *The Report of the Working Party of the Arts Council of Great Britain* concluded in 1968, the nature of obscenity law in Britain was such that "even a morally innocent transgressor cannot ascertain *in advance* whether he will have transgressed it or not, so that . . . ignorance of the law . . . is imposed upon him by the nature of the law" (242, my italics; hereafter cited as *Arts Council Report*). In 1970, the *Commission on Pornography and Obscenity* noted that in the United States it "is impossible for a publisher, retailer or exhibitor to know in advance whether he will be charged with a criminal offence for distributing a particular work . . ." (*The Report of the Commission on Obscenity and Pornography,* 45; hereafter referred to as *Presidential Commission*).

So even if individuals believe in their own minds that terms like obscenity definitely do describe something and that they of course know what it is, there is still no legal agreement as to what it might be. There exist no clear legal standards regarding illicit expression because the law itself cannot define terms like *obscenity,* nor even the terms like *deprave, corrupt, indecent* or *disgusting* which are often added in an effort to better pin down what obscenity means, but finally offer no clear help. As *The Arts Council Report* observed,"no two people [in England] can be counted on to agree what is or is not obscene. . . . [Moreover no] definition has ever been offered to show what was meant by depravity or corruption. . . . [One] inscrutable phrase has been resorted to in explanation of another" (222), and as if to illustrate that very point, *Regina v. Butler* (1992) noted that the Canadian "Criminal Code did not provide a definition of any of the operative terms, 'obscene,' 'indecent,' or 'disgusting.'"

So it is not merely legal experts or the opponents of censorship who alone keep complaining about this confusion. It is the judges themselves who repeatedly recognize it, and they admit to the problem even as they continue to rule against various writers, speakers, and publishers: Justice Brennan himself noted that terms like *obscenity* "do not mean the same thing to all people, all the time, everywhere." After reviewing the history of censorship rulings he concluded: "Many [legal] decisions have recognized that these terms of obscenity statutes are not precise" (*Roth v. United States*, 1956). And Judge Jerome Frank remarked that a "standard so difficult for our ablest judges to interpret is hardly precise" (*Roth v. Goldman 1949*). Even a Supreme Court Justice, like Potter Stewart, had to admit that he himself perhaps could "never succeed in intelligibly" defining pornography, but, he sought to assure everyone, "I know it when I see it" (*Jacobellis v. Ohio,* 1964). Brennan later alluded to the now famous non-definition by observing that "although we have assumed that obscenity does exist and that we 'know it when [we] see it' . . . , we are manifestly unable to describe it in advance except by reference to concepts so elusive that they fail to distinguish clearly between protected and unprotected speech . . . ." The "vagueness of the standards in the obscenity area," he added, compelled "persons to guess . . . whether their conduct is covered by a criminal statute" and the "resulting uncertainty is utterly intolerable . . . because it invites arbitrary and erratic enforcement of the law . . ." (*Paris Adult Theatre I v. Slaton,* 1973)

But when it comes to present-day confusion there is nothing extraordinary about the vagueness of contemporary standards regarding obscenity or pornography. For the absence of clear standards and the consequent *ex post facto* nature of legal judgments--I cannot define what it is, but I know it when I see it; be sure not to print what twelve countrymen might later find blameable--has historically tended to be a defining characteristic of censorship involving all variety of expression. In Anglo-American law the crime of "seditious libel" pertained to criticism of the government and its officials, but what constituted seditious libel was not generally defined, but was determined by a judge or jury on a case by case basis by means of the arrest, trial, and conviction of various authors and publishers. Similarly, as Leonard Levy has pointed out, "Blasphemy was a unique crime in the sense that no one could know whether it had been committed until a jury rendered its verdict. . . . In the case of blasphemy [unlike any other crime not involving expression], the defendant could be wholly unaware of his guilt until charged and convicted" (489). And when in 1993 the Supreme Court of the United States sought to censor sexually hostile expression in the workplace the same confusion emerged. Justice O'Conner, writing for the majority, admitted that defining hostile expression "is not, and by its nature cannot be, a mathematically precise test," but it may be said to exist so "long as the environment would reasonably be perceived, and is perceived, as hostile." In other words, the court could not reasonably define what hostility was but assured everyone that reasonable people would know it when they perceived it.

Though concurring with the decision, Justice Scalia complained that the term "hostile . . . does not seem to be a very clear standard" and that as such it would leave "virtually unguided juries" with little "notion of what the vague word means." But what definition used to limit expression ever did offer clear guidance to judges or juries? None that the *Arts Council Report* could find. They similarly noted that jurors in Great Britain also had to decide obscenity cases "with no possible guidance" as to what terms such as "artistic merit" or "to deprave and corrupt" mean or imply (233), and *The Presidential Commission on Obscenity and Pornography* found that "[n]one of the federal statutes generally prohibiting the distribution of 'obscene' material defines the term" (43). The result is that in censorship trials juries tend to remain not merely unguided, but they are put in a position of formulating law as the need arises. The verdict of the jury in obscenity trials, Judge Learned Hand quipped, "is not the conclusion of a syllogism of which they are to find only the minor premise, but really a small bit of legislation *ad hoc*" (qtd. in Alpert 53). If, as noted in *Regina v. Butler,* "it is not the judicial function to define the material or actions which are to be proscribed by law," that function when it comes to censorship trials has traditionally been left to the judiciary, to judges and juries, because of the regular failure of legislatures to provide them with well-defined criteria and standards.

The impression most people have is that though judges and other authorities often fail to clearly define illicit expression, the censor wishes at least to try and define it and would in fact benefit from any successful attempt to put forth a clear definition of what constitutes objectionable material. But vague wording and the absence of clear standards has been such a persistent characteristic of censorship statutes for so long that one begins to suspect that the absence of reasonable definition is something censors regard not as a problem to be rectified, but as an advantage they can exploit.

In 1923 the League of Nations convened a conference in Geneva on "The Suppression of the Circulation and Traffic in Obscene Publications." One Greek delegate suggested that they ought to define the meaning of obscene before proceeding. Sir Archibald Bodkin, the British Director of Public Prosecutions, pointed out that "there is no definition of indecent or obscene in English Statute Law," and everyone agreed that "no definition was possible" and then proceeded with their work (reported in Causton 55-6). Perhaps they had been swayed by Sir Bodkin's warning "against any attempt at a definition [of obscenity] lest it restrict his ability to prosecute what he did not like" (Thompson 18). And in Soviet Russia, the "vague and inexact formulation" of a 1935 law regarding pornography "enabled the authorities to institute criminal proceedings and imprison people on the most ridiculous charges" (Kon 73); while in the 1980's in the United States, Andrea Dworkin and Catherine Mackinnon, drafted a so-called model pornography law. It sought to cast as wide a net as possible and "defined" pornography through a myriad confusion of terms and conditions (see below for a partial list), adding afterward that it "shall not be a defense that the defendant . . . did not know nor intend that the materials were pornography . . . ." This is no reminder that ignorance of the law is no excuse, for it does not say that no one shall be excused for not knowing that pornography is illegal, but rather that no one shall be excused for not knowing what pornography is. The statement is as revealing a reflection upon the nature and application of censorship law as one might get. It readily admits the fact that their so-called model law remains unclear as to what constitutes illicit expression, and it takes that fact into account not by way of confessing a fault in the law, but in order to insist that the failure of the lawmakers to make clear what we should understand illicit expression to be shall be no defense for the accused who, given the nature of the law, may very well know that pornography is illegal but is not likely to clearly understand what constitutes pornography.

There remain good practical reasons for this recurrent absence of clear definitions and standards. It means that illicit expression becomes in practice whatever governments wish at any particular time and place to characterize without clear prior notice as illicit expression for the purpose of arresting whomever governments decide is undesirable. Testifying before the House Select Committee on Current Pornographic Materials in 1952 a New York police captain expressed his bewilderment at trying to determine what obscenity defined: "The thing is so nebulous that we, as law-enforcement officers, don't know whether we are coming or going." But the practical fact of the matter is that the very nebulousness of the law has allowed police to come and go as they please, seizing publications or arresting "undesirables" or harassing countless booksellers with arbitrary prosecutions which often drive them into bankruptcy having to defend themselves. The aim of arbitrary power is to rule arbitrarily, and those laws "defining" elicit expression remain some of the sharpest weapons arbitrary power can utilize and wield when it feels threatened or just takes a dislike to some otherwise innocent subject. So, after reviewing the legal definitions of obscenity which have come to us down through the centuries, one may with only slight exaggeration and a touch of irony offer the following definition: *Censorship law is that law which covers illicit expression and which characteristically and probably often by design does not know, cannot define or formulate, and fails to publicize what illicit expression is.*

In the next section I will suggest what terms like obscenity and pornography do define, and that the reason people can't identify what they mean is that almost everyone on all sides of the debate tends for the wrong reasons to look in the wrong places. For the moment we might recall that clear legal standards function not only to serve notice to citizens, but to place restraints upon governments and government agents as well. They have served to replace the unlimited, arbitrary power of men with the limiting rule of law. The absence of clear, uniform standards of law which apply equally to all citizens was and is a defining characteristic of autocratic rule in both pre-modern societies and modern despotic and totalitarian states, and the men who formulated the principles of modern liberal democracy called first and foremost for clear standards of law in reaction to the common practice of arbitrary rule. "The Freedom of Men under Government," John Locke wrote in his *Second Treatise of Government*, "is to have a standing Rule to live by, common to everyone of that Society . . . ." Accordingly the Due Process Claus of the Fourteenth Amendment to the U.S. Constitution requires that all criminal law provide fair notice as to what the State commands or forbids. "I was taught in law school that people are entitled to know what it is they may be prosecuted for," Chief Judge Dolores Sloviter noted when complaining about the vagueness of terms like "indecency" in the Computer Decency Act (in a hearing conducted to determine that Act's constitutionality, May 10, 1996). But the successful struggle to have citizens live securely under the rule of standing laws so that they know what they may be prosecuted for has generally by-passed censorship statutes. The "nature and history of obscenity" up until present time is nothing like "the fundamental laws of property, of crimes like murder, rape, and theft, or even of negligence, whose meaning has remained relatively constant. That of obscenity has frequently changed, almost from decade to decade within the past century . . ." (Judge Curtis Bok, *Commonwealth of Pennsylvania v. Gordon et al*, 1949). According to one legal expert who reported to The Arts Council committee, "Obscenity is incapable of objective definition and is therefore an unsatisfactory subject for the criminal law" (223).

Why this confusion of meaning? Why the continuous presentation and revision of differing definitions? Why the absence of clear legal standards to guide citizens, judges and juries? Why is it that in criminal law the definition of robbery or murder, having been set down by legislative bodies, is clear to any judge or jury, but when it comes to crimes like obscenity we remain incapable of coming up with an objective definition? The answer is indeed as the Arts Council concluded that obscenity truly is incapable of objective definition, and the reason for that is, as we have been noting, that obscenity deals with opinion and not objective facts. But how did we come to this impasse in the first place?

If as Lord Devlin noted, juries in obscenity trials must indeed determine what morality means, this does not simply place an unusual burden on twelve men and women, making, as Judge Hand remarked, legislators out of jurors. In addition and more fundamentally, the heart of the problem is that asking a jury to arrive at verdicts of this particular kind violates "the original purpose of a jury [which] was to decide facts, not make decisions involving opinions" (Lord Goodman, *London Daily Telegraph*, August 7, 1968). Geoffrey Robertson has explained the nature of this problem quite penetratingly:

> The basic problem with any obscenity law which applies a legal test to methods of expression is that it calls for a judgement of *opinion* rather than a finding of fact. . . . Thus obscenity trials reflect the inability of traditional modes of criminal adjudication to comprehend the issues which can arise in the decision to censor. Criminal law has developed a method for obtaining the truth in a world of fingerprints, alibis, police informers, bloodstains, and the dog that doesn't bark in the night. These are facts able to be tested. . . . The machinery of the criminal law is geared to adjudicate disputes about *facts*. Obscenity cases call for decision, not about truth or falsity, but about which of two plausible opinions is to be preferred. (197)

In a murder trial, the jury knows that a crime has been committed, and it must determine whether in fact the accused committed it. In an obscenity trial it is a quite different matter. The jury already knows for a fact that the accused actually did make a speech or print a pamp' 'et. and what they have to determine, in these cases, is whether *in their opinion* that constitutes a crime.

I have suggested earlier that the reason nobody can agree upon what obscenity means is that there really is no such *thing* as obscenity. There are, we might now say, no facts upon which to make such a judgment. Lawmakers and judges may juggle terms around, sometimes changing old ones, sometimes adding new ones, and all along what they say strikes us as intelligible, and often for that reason alone people feel or say they know what obscenity actually is when in fact all ey really know is what the term obscenity means. In other words, whe ney say they know what obscenity is they are usually mistaking clarity of definition to mean that some actual thing or occurrence has been clearly, accurately and truly identified. That any of the above definitions we have seen may be called "clear" means only that they are intelligible, and just because someone readily understands these or other statements does not mean that they therefore correspond to anything which has an objective existence. The statements "milk is black" and "apples are blue" are clear enough, even a child could understand them, but no sensible adult and very few children would conclude from the clear meaning of the statement that such things are true--that there exists in the factual world we all experience anything like black milk or blue apples. Yet when one person (or twelve persons) says he or she knows what obscenity is, he or she is usually merely saying that they understand the meaning of the legal definition and can, if asked, state it clearly for you, and in this case they quite often mistake the intelligibility of the statement to mean that it therefore actually refers to something.

The bottom line is that when we speak of things like *obscenity*, or *community standards*, or *depravity*, we are more often than not quite literally talking nonsense and don't realize it. This is not to say that this is all silly and stupid stuff (which it probably is), but that most all legal definitions about obscenity and the like are nonsense for the reason that they are statements which presume and appear to refer to facts, but which never really do for the reason that *they are not statements that can be tested against any facts*. They consist of statements that can never be factually verified or refuted. Obscenity is not really something that can be proved, certainly not as a matter of fact, and thus judges and juries, lacking not simply clear legal standards, but *testable criteria* for establishing whether a crime has in fact been committed, must necessarily fall back upon opinion and all the problems and disagreements that come with it. Legal definitions of obscenity are nonsense for the reason that they can neither be verified nor refuted as a matter of fact.

Take the famous *Hicklin Test* (qtd. and discussed below). Lord Cockburn in 1867 (*Regina v. Hicklin)* indicated that the "test" of obscenity was the tendency of a work to "corrupt and deprave." It sounded good enough to become the defining statement on obscenity throughout Anglo-American law for a century. But how does one test for corruption and depravity in a person, let alone the signs of the tendency to corrupt persons which may presumably be found in a work of literature? What physical evidence does one look for, what empirical evidence should one seek to discover? What are we supposed to observe when we wish to find the tendency to deprave in a work? Not only do the legal definitions give little or no clear indication of what to look for, but to make matters worse they repeatedly insist that proof of actual harm is not required to convict for obscenity.

The last point will be the subject in and of itself of discussion to follow, but it is relevant to the present issue. The precedent-setting case for modern obscenity law occurred with the conviction of Edmund Curll in 1728. The most significant single aspect of that case was the court's acceptance of the Attorney General of England's contention that Curll was liable under English common law because even though no physical harm could be said to result from his publication, "peace may be broken in many instances without an actual force." Thus the issue of physical harm was removed from consideration in modern censorship law (the major point of upcoming discussion). And in major censorship rulings the courts continued to insist upon its irrelevance. For example in *Roth v. The United States,* the Supreme Court ruled that "convictions may be had without proof that obscene material will create perceptibly clear and present danger" and in *Regina v.Butler,* the Supreme Court of Canada ruled that outlawing pornography "does not demand actual proof of harm" (both rulings are quoted and discussed at greater length later).

The significance of the Curll conviction is not simply that it was gotten without proof of actual harm, but more fundamentally, in ruling physical force from consideration in obscenity trials, the court established that convictions for obscenity could be had without factual evidence. For if there need not be evidence of actual force, there need not be--in fact probably cannot be--evidence of perceptible physical effects. That is how we got to the present impasse: *the common law courts in early eighteenth century England effectively threw out factual evidence as a basis for arriving at censorship decisions.*

This has proved anything but a stumbling block for prosecutors. For not having to present factual evidence, but only the possibility of a "tendency" or a violation of "community standards" prosecutors are relieved of a considerable burden of proof and judges and juries are left with no real hard evidence to go on. And those who agitate for censorship realize full well that the absence of evidence presents no real problem, certainly not in a court of law or when preaching to those who accept conventional folk wisdom without regard for the facts.

When it comes to censorship, facts constitute a nuisance that needs to be ignored. In the absence of proof one can always resort to stipulative definitions, as Catherine Itzen does when she states, "There still persists the 'illusion' that there is no provable connection between pornography and violence . . . The truth . . . is that pornography *is* violence" (43). Itzin's two statements about pornography are quite revealing. Philosophers, at least since David Hume over two hundred years ago, have distinguished between verifiable (sometimes "testable") statements and nonverifiable (sometimes "nonsense") statements. Itzin gives us good examples of both. The statement that there is a connection between pornography and violence is verifiable (as being either true or false). It purports to correspond to a set of facts which could support or refute the statement. The statement that pornography is violence is on the order of "Truth is beauty, beauty truth." It is nonsense--a stipulative and arbitrarily assigned definition that no amount of research into facts of any kind could possibly support or refute, even though the statement purports and may appear to many to be something that could conceivably correspond to an objective world of factual information.

Notice as well that Itzin prefers to argue from the nonsense rather than the verifiable statement. She says that there is a persistent "illusion" that no provable connection between pornography and violence exists, but she does not then attempt, as one might expect from such a statement, to disillusion us by proving the connection, or showing that the data were not gotten or interpreted correctly. There is not even a call for further research into a world of objective facts that might prove her contentions about the evils of pornography. There is instead merely the setting aside of any and all verifiable statements in favor of what is literally nonsense. In this she typifies the response of the censor to the absence of supporting evidence. In a somewhat similar manner Julienne Dickey and Gail Chester point out that "we [feminists] need to be quite clear that there is little *scientific* evidence [for the argument that pornography causes harm]. We have to use other, *feminist* arguments" (5). Again, the problem that there is no scientific evidence is not confronted with a call to review the data or seek out new evidence, certainly not with an admission that one's argument may in fact be entirely unfounded and needs to be seriously modified, if not abandoned entirely.   If the problem is that an argument has no scientific basis, why replace it with a feminist argument, unless an argument not based upon evidence is preferable to one that seeks to be?

Perhaps Mary Whitehouse, leader of England's National Viewers and Listeners Association, put it best when she addressed the 1987 Conservative Party Conference: "you've got to get away from this silly business of having to prove things," she advised.   But that is precisely the significance of the *Curll* conviction.   It established what is arguably the most important precedent in modern censorship law.   For by saying that harm could occur without evidence of actual force *Curll* got the criminal courts away from the business of having to prove things. That is the reason why everyone, including judges and juries for hundreds of years now, has been struggling unsuccessfully to define illicit expression.   There is, according to the legal standards *Curll* established, no actual thing to refer to, no facts that can be presented to support the charge that something is obscene or indecent or corrupting.   And since the eighteenth century the courts have continued to rule out legal definitions of illicit expression which could conceivably make sense, that is to say, statements regarding the nature and consequences of illicit expression which could be tested against the facts in a court of law or elsewhere.   Thus what we have on the one hand are testable statements regarding illicit expression and the fact that most all studies have shown that various forms of illicit expression do not present a danger to society or individuals.   However these statements and the conclusions research has drawn from them have consistently been ruled to be irrelevant to the issue of censorship (see upcoming section for a discussion of these conclusions). Consequently what we therefore get in their place are nonsense definitions of illicit expression which no one can ever verify or refute.   Censorship has thrived for centuries precisely because it dismisses testable statements and the conclusions derived from them as irrelevant and replaces fact with opinion, clear definition with assumptions which neither have nor can have any factual relevance:

Gentleman: "Excuse me, my good man, could you call me a cab?"
Young man: "O.K. You're a cab."

Stating that pornography is violence no more makes it true than calling a man a cab makes him a cab.   "Existence is not a predicate," Kant tried to warn us. Simply because we can predicate something in a sentence does mean that thing truly has existence.   But that is what definitions of obscenity or pornography repeatedly do, predicate that obscenity is this or pornography that without reference to any possible factual evidence to test and verify the truth of the statement, offering only the stipulative definition that these things are real and true or what is more correct that twelve people *believe* it is true, and it can be "proven" in a court of law without the introduction of empirical evidence. They predicate a whole set of arbitrary definitions and then would have us accept that such things really do exist or occur in the real world where things like real crimes like rape or robbery do in fact really occur. No matter what one is talking about, without the requirement that one should test any of one's assertions or statements against the facts, there remains no controls or limits upon what nonsense one may utter.   Remove such limitations from criminal trials, and there remains little or no control over the number of convictions that can be had of otherwise harmless citizens. We know what a thief is before we even see one because the legal definition is based upon facts that need to occur for someone to be convicted of thievery, and an accused individual will be convicted of thievery only if the facts prove him a thief. We know pornography only when we see it and everyone sees it differently because pornography remains a matter of opinion and not fact. And once opinion changes, a good book becomes pornography or a bad book becomes a modern classic, and honest citizens can become criminals when enough people are of the *opinion* that they are or should be.   There used to be a legal procedure known as *compurgation* whereby a person could be acquitted of a charge if he could bring forth enough people who would swear, not that they had knowledge that he was not guilty, but that they did not *believe* he stood guilty of the crime he was accused of. The procedure was becoming archaic already by the seventeenth century and in the nineteenth it was removed from the English legal code. Yet the archaic procedure persists in censorship cases where not acquittal only but conviction as well may be had if people can be gotten to *believe* that one or another opinion regarding the accused is correct.

Censorship may be about crimes, but it is certainly not about facts. It is about crimes of opinions or belief, and necessarily so. For without actual facts to base a decision on, one has only opinions to go on. So long as these are the conditions under which censorship trials operate one has no legal right to expect invariable, objective standards.

Few nowadays in modern constitutional democracies would agree to the prosecution of individuals for offences so vague that not even a high court justice can intelligibly define them, nor would many people likely accept the rulings of any judge who had said, "I cannot define what robbery is, but I know a thief when I see one"? But when it comes to matters of obscenity we are prepared to free men from the limits law ordinarily places upon government officers and citizens within democracies.   The successful application and fair enforcement of any law requires a high degree of specificity as to what defines and constitutes criminal action so as to clearly inform the citizenry, limit and control police action, and guide judges and juries. It is not unreasonable to expect that censorship be constrained by the same clearly defined rules of law so that, as *The Presidential Commission* recommended, "those subject to the law could know in advance what materials were prohibited and so that judicial decisions would not be based upon the subjective reactions of particular judges or jurors" (47). But such is not the case. When it comes to obscenity we are prepared to grant extraordinary exceptions to the rules of law. We readily tolerate the rule of men and accept vague statutes in the belief that, even though the law fails to define the crime, one man will know it when he sees it or even that twelve people we assume to be reasonable will know it. "A magistrate," G. B Shaw noted, "has laws to administer: a censor has nothing but his own opinion. . . . [N]o man is lawfully at the mercy of the magistrate's personal caprice, prejudice, ignorance, superstition, temper, stupidity, resentment, timidity, ambition, or private conviction. . . . [T]he criminal and the judge stand in the presence of a law that binds them both equally . . . ." But a writer, to the contrary, is "at the personal mercy of the Censor" (Preface to *Blanco Posnet)*.

Even though neither lawmakers, jurists, nor ordinary citizens are capable of defining the rules regarding illicit expression--one indicator that such regulations are remnants within democracies of the kind of autocratic rule governing pre-modern societies--that fact has rarely persuaded those who ordinarily oppose arbitrary justice in all other matters to reject its enforcement when it pertains to expression.

"Someone must have traduced Joseph K. For without having done anything wrong he was arrested one morning." So begins Franz Kafka's novel, *The Trial*. There is a written constitution in K's country, and every one of its citizens accepts the law. But not Joseph K. He seems to be lacking common sense. For he spends the entire novel unsuccessfully seeking to gain access to the law, to try and come to some rational understanding of its meaning and application, particularly as it applies to him, since no one seems willing or able to tell him after his arrest what he has done wrong. Readers and scholars have puzzled for decades over this marvelous parable of the modern condition. I know it sounds farfetched, but maybe Joseph K. was being charged with obscenity.

Chapter 2

A Matter of Class

In censorship cases, modern liberal democracies continue to enact the kind of arbitrary justice common to pre-modern societies. Moreover, when it is a matter of censorship, democracies otherwise committed to equal justice under law also do not feel compelled to reject laws which are not "common to everyone." Censorship is motivated by class fear and class prejudice, and censorship law, even within so-called democracies, continues to function as a means of legitimizing those fears and prejudices. Thus while conviction and sentencing have been shown to vary on the basis of race, class, or gender (see, e.g., the case presented to the U.S. Supreme Court in *McClesky v. Kemp*, 1987), the laws themselves do not ordinarily make distinctions according to them. That is clearly not the case with censorship law. It specifically and explicitly discriminates on the basis of class, even within democracies claiming to uphold the principle of equal justice under law. *The Obscene and Indecent Publications Act* of New South Wales, for example, re-iterated the position of legislatures throughout the British Commonwealth in the first half of the twentieth century. In setting forth the "meaning of obscene and indecent," it stated: "In determining for the purposes of this Act whether any publication . . . is obscene the court shall have regard to . . . the persons, class of persons and age groups" to whom the publication was intended, and the publication "shall be held to be obscene when it tends or is likely in any manner to deprave, corrupt or injure the morals of . . . the persons in any such class or age groups, notwithstanding that persons in other classes or age groups may not be similarly affected" (recorded in St. John-Stevas 221-2).

The determination of obscenity on the basis of class was a hallmark of British and American law for a hundred years and more, due in large part to the influence of "the Hicklin test": In *Regina vs. Hicklin* (1867), Lord Cockburn said, "I think the test of obscenity is this, whether the tendency of the matter charged as obscenity is to deprave and corrupt those whose minds are open to such immoral influences, and into whose hands a publication of this sort may fall." We can infer from the judge's words the scenario censors imagine and fear: Material which the lord of the manor may read with impunity may fall into the hands of the maid or gardener whose minds, unlike his, are presumed to be more open to depraving immoral influences. The Hicklin test offered nothing new, but merely codified a prevalent prejudice. The "test" for blasphemy had been no different: In *Regina v. Hetherington*, 1840, the bookseller, Hetherington, was convicted for publishing an attack upon the Old Testament because he was "careless of the effect it might have on the morals of the unthinking working class."

A major reason why no one seems able to define something like pornography on the basis of content is that obscenity law itself says that the very same material which is harmless, bawdy stuff when sitting on the night stand of some aristocrat becomes pornography only when it falls into the hands of the lower classes. Thus in pre-revolutionary France, books could be legal or illegal or registered as "permitted only for persons who are very well known" (Darnton 4). Uncertainty as to what in and of itself constitutes unclean publications has not been matched by any uncertainty regarding exactly what kind of people will be corrupted by it. For centuries no one has been able to define precisely what obscenity is, but during all this time just about everyone has remained confident that, whatever it may be, it "is a corruptive social influence" whose "repression is necessary," but not because everyone is open to its corrupting influence but because it "seems to hold a permanent attraction *for a portion of humanity*" (John Courtney Murray, qtd. in Kendrick 205, my italics). Both the layman and the judge may not be able to tell us what distinguishes art from obscenity, but they clearly know and have shown themselves quite capable over and again of identifying without much difficulty who within the general population should not be exposed to obscenity. They can with little difficulty distinguish those "whose minds are open to . . . immoral influences" from a privileged few who can read whatever they like with impunity because of their supposedly superior moral qualities. Anthony Comstock's constant exposure to "corrupting" material somehow did not corrupt him, probably because it could not corrupt anybody, but that of course was not what Comstock and his followers believed. His familiarity with evil and ruinous literature did not "endanger his own moral nature. Comstock worked for many years in a sewer, as he himself described it, but he came up every now and then and went to prayer meetings, where he was accepted as devout and uncontaminated." His incorruptibility might have "afforded living proof of the staunchness of the human soul in resisting the evil suggestions of the most vicious fictionists" (Broun 272 & 268). It proved instead that a few good men like Comstock were invulnerable to evils whose contamination the souls of ordinary men were not capable of resisting. This same kind of exceptional invulnerability apparently also exists throughout the British police force, since in *Regina v. Clayton and Halsey*, 1962, the Courts established that no amount of exposure to pornography could deprave a policeman (*Arts Council Report* 227). On the other hand once we have identified or wish to identify a person or class of people as corrupt, then their uncontrollable susceptibility to the corrupting influence of literature is taken for granted, and no amount of precaution seems too foolish: By 1782 the Marquis de Sade's sexual proclivities were clearly established and notorious enough for him to have been locked up for four years of a twelve year imprisonment, yet the prison warden refused him the books he wanted because, as his wife wrote, he told her that "all your books have been taken away because they inflamed your mind and caused you to write unseemly things" (qtd. in Lever 341).

More recently Pete Hamill writing in *Playboy* wondered, If it is true that "human beings are so weak and pornography so powerful" then why, "having pored over more pornography than the ordinary man sees in a lifetime," weren't "MacKinnon and Dworkin playing the Kraft-Ebbing Music Hall with the rest of the perverts?" The reason is that the power which pornography or any form of illicit expression is thought to posses is believed to be selective and discriminating and the moral superiority of those who monitor all that is vile and polluting places them, as Hamill put it, "beyond contamination" (188).

Just as men believed torture could discover a witch because witches responded to torture differently from innocent mortals, so do women like Dworkin and MacKinnon believe that pornography serves to expose the weakness and inferiority of men in modern society. The reason MacKinnon and Dworkin are not corrupted by what they contend drives men to madness and cruelty is that in their view the ordinary man is a pervert, or a potential pervert, and every ordinary woman is an innocent victim. The fact that pornography does not appear to captivate women to the extent it does men is taken as proof of the power of pornography, not simply to corrupt, but perhaps more importantly, to identify for Dworkin, MacKinnon and their followers those in society who are most prone to corruption.

In the final analysis it is not the expression which poses the perceived threat, but its audience, and censors can live with uncertainty regarding the defining characteristics of things like obscenity or profanity because censorship functions to define characteristics we ought to be wary of when we find them, not in expression, but in people. *Censorship functions to define people rather than expression.* That is why terms like obscenity are vague and uncertain when we try to understand them as identifying characteristics of expression rather than as ciphers used to stigmatize people. Censorship's ultimate purpose is to categorize types of expression as illicit primarily as a means of marking classes of people within society as inferior or dangerous: traditionally women, but most recently men, children, the poor and lower classes in general, racial, religious and sexual minorities, resident aliens, and so on. It functions, not primarily as the censor claims, to protect moral and religious values by identifying expression that is supposed to be blasphemous and immoral, but to maintain and validate political control and social hierarchies by identifying classes of people government and society needs to guard against and restrain. The nature and content of the material does not matter so much as the need to establish or reinforce what Susan Sontag has called a "hierarchy of competence" (72). At the top, reside a privileged class of persons of such distinct virtue and character that they can view material which would be harmful to most others. At the bottom, exist a class of people whose intellectual, emotional, and moral character is so flawed and untrustworthy that, in the interest of social order, they cannot be permitted to lead uncontrolled lives. Just who these privileged and incompetent people are will vary depending of course on who makes and enforces the laws and who the laws aim to benefit or control. According to one nineteenth-century reviewer of a book on prostitution, above everyone else in the general population one may find the "scientific investigator," the "*litterateur*" and the "really good" person who may view "photographic representations of filth and low debauchery" unharmed and who may even be motivated by such representations to seek "the amelioration of vice," while on the bottom of the social scale exist "the sensual, the vicious, the young and inexperienced" for whom the very same material is "too liable to be converted into mere guidebooks to vice, or to afford amusement to the prurient fancy of the depraved." Or there are judges such as Morgan J. O'Brien and those who in the Judge's opinion posses a "common and vulgar mind," a "class of people from whom unclean publications ought to be withheld" (qtd. in Kendrick 27 &175. Kendrick's book, among its many other virtues, is a most important study of the class bias underlying modern censorship practices.).

Victorian patriarchs sought to protect impressionable women from erotic literature that would seduce them into a life of sin and degradation, and in our own day a number of self-proclaimed feminists have called for censoring erotic literature which has the power to drive impressionable men to rape and violence. In each case the intent is the same, not to stigmatize expression, but to denigrate women or demonize men for the purpose of characterizing a class of individuals within society as possessing a diminished capacity for distinguishing fantasy from reality or right from wrong.

There are of course rare *individuals* who cannot tell fantasy from reality or right from wrong, and we do have names for them. They are called psychotics or the criminally insane, but there is no reason whatsoever to believe that these characteristics are more pronounced or grouped especially in certain classes of people--that women or men as a class are more prone to psychosis, that the sensual are more vicious or the vulgar more depraved. The most egregious error censors make is not to mistake art for smut, but to attribute to whole classes of normal, law-abiding citizens the identifying characteristics of individuals who suffer from mental and other degenerative disorders. Discussions and rulings respecting illicit expression are littered with these observations about people arrived at on the basis of stereotypes, prejudices, superstitions, and ideological intolerance. That I suspect is one major reason why the so-called Hicklin test for obscenity was so influential. It was not only not a test for literature, but it was actually no test at all. It contains no recommendation as to how one might on a case by case basis test the proposition which is at the heart of the ruling that some classes of people are more susceptible to immoral influence than others, and no tests were ever conducted. It merely formulated a prevailing prejudice regarding class differences and recommended that obscenity rulings be guided by it, as they in fact had been and would continue to be.

But the practical fact of the matter is that judges could not and indeed did not take at face value the tests for obscenity they, following Cockburn, proposed. If they did it would require that obscenity rulings be determined not by incorruptible judges of moral character so high that they remain immune to the depraving influence of obscene expression. Most appropriately, obscenity rulings would have to come from those whose minds are in fact open to immoral influences. The ultimate paradox of the tests for obscenity judges keep referring to is that if obscene material harms some and not others, then the wrong people are handing down the rulings, or at least those who do rule for us find themselves in an absurd, contradictory position. How exactly does a Supreme Court Justice like Potter Stewart know pornography when he sees it? Does it stimulate certain physiological responses normal to healthy males; does it arouse his prurient interest or appeal to "the widespread weakness for titillation by pornography" that Justice Brennan would later refer to? If it doesn't, then he would have to rule that the material is not prurient and pornographic? If it does, then he would conclude that it is, but then he would identify himself, a Justice of the Supreme Court of the United States, as no different from anyone else when it comes to pornography, and that can't be. Or if the judge recognizes pornography when he sees it but is not thereby driven to a life of depravity and crime, then he might have to rule that for all practical purposes sexually arousing material is in fact harmless stuff that has no immoral influence, and that can't be either.

Given the prejudices that obscenity rulings serve to enforce, that there is no common human nature, that classes of people within any society can be identified as clearly inferior, particularly when compared to certain social elites, and that one significant measure of that inferiority is their susceptibility to corruption as a result of what they see and hear--given these presumptions then the difficulty judges face in censorship rulings is that they must assume effects they themselves do not experience occurring to people who are not at all like them. Much of the hesitancy and uncertainty in judicial decisions derives, I suspect, from this difficulty. We do not regularly read that obscenity is that which "has been shown to," "has been proven to," "is known to." Instead obscenity is defined as that which "might," or "has a tendency to." It is not simply the fact that evidence of harmful effects is lacking which accounts for the uncertain wording in these rulings, but that those handing down obscenity rulings cannot state that certain material is in fact known to corrupt without risking implicating themselves among the victims and undermining the very class differences which censorship law, independent of any prosecutions, but in its very wording, serves to reinforce.

Then again defining obscenity in terms of "a tendency" a work may have to produce this or that harmful effect gives the government open season on practically any work it chooses to censor, since nothing is immune to misuse and abuse, not even the best of things, like let's say the Bible which has been used throughout history to justify more bloodshed than perhaps any other single work. No one can argue against the censors that any work or person does not possess a tendency to harm. It would be a no-win argument. One can't even argue against those feminists who say that every man is a potential rapist. One might even add to that he is also a potential robber, murderer, or saint for that matter. But that is certainly no reason to arrest anyone or to keep them from reading what they want. If we are going to restrain any one person for that reason, we would have to restrain everyone from doing just about anything, which is what totalitarian societies are famous for. The potential for good or evil in a person or a work is practically unlimited, and for that and other reasons largely indeterminable. Were we were to arrest and prosecute people for their *tendency* to harm, no citizen could claim innocence. To say that a work or person has a tendency to harm is not to make clearly erroneous statements about the person or work. It is probably more likely true than not, but it does serve to deny the legal presumption of innocence and make every citizen and every utterance guilty before the fact.

As Lord Littleton noted: "To argue against any breach of liberty from the ill use that may be made of it is to argue against liberty itself, since all is capable of being abused" (qtd. in Nelson 286). That is why the modern liberal tradition has insisted that the law "may punish the *overt acts*, but not the tendency, which is not actually hurtful . . . . Punishing a man for the tendency of his *principles* is punishing him *before* he is guilty, for fear he *should be guilty*." (Dr. Furneaux's published letter to Blackstone, qtd. in Nelson 56). As Jefferson put it in his *Statute of Virginia for Religious Freedom*: "to suffer the civil magistrate to intrude his powers into the field of opinion and to restrain the profession or propagation of principles on supposition of their ill tendency is a dangerous fallacy . . . . [I]t is time enough, for the rightful purposes of civil government, for its officers to interfere when principles break out into overt acts against peace and good order" (Dumbauld 35).

Censorship in modern liberal, constitutional democracies succeeds in violation of principles basic to modern liberal democracies by defining illicit expression after the fact and presuming guilt before the fact. In large part the right of the government to punish on the basis of "tendency" came about, as we shall see, from the fact that modern censorship law eliminated altogether from consideration the question of actual harm resulting from overt acts; but in any event, to permit governments to prosecute and punish any person on the basis of the tendency he might posses regardless of the fact that he has actually done no wrong or to censor any work for that reason is to permit the prosecution of anyone whom government or society finds objectionable or offensive without evidence of actual harm, and that as we shall see is by legal definition exactly what obscenity is all about. Yet even were the civil magistrates not to intrude to the extent of arresting persons for the expression of opinion, merely to state that the government has the right to prosecute people on the bases of tendencies serves the purpose of marking as dangerous or inferior classes of people who hold or might hold certain opinions or who posses or are assumed to posses certain character traits. Statutes that target tendencies rather than overt acts not only give the government wide intrusive powers, but they allow it to stigmatize for society classes of persons, like for instance communists or atheists, whom society must guard against even if no prosecution of such persons were ever to occur. They operate similarly to those statutes on the books which in many states are rarely enforced, but whose existence serves an important notice. Even if no person were ever arrested, or tried, or convicted, the mere existence of the laws pertaining to sodomy, or miscegenation, or fornication, serve to stigmatize select groups of people and to reinforce prejudice and discrimination against them.

Of course we cannot finally expect that people whose minds are truly corrupted by obscenity should actually rule on it, but that is not because we would not want such people serving as judges, but because such people simply do not exist. They are inventions, like witches and warlocks, or the commies which Sen. Joseph McCarthy claimed existed in every branch of government (he never found one). They are imagined for the purpose of giving exceptional power to some, justifying arbitrary social controls, and imposing cruel and unusual punishments upon those who do not conform to the predominant ideology of a particular time and place.

Chapter 3

Mass Communication

Because censorship exists for the purpose of justifying, maintaining and enforcing class distinctions, when determining illicit expression, it is not the information itself which worries the authorities and moves them to act, but its dissemination, particularly the massive distribution of information formerly reserved for an exclusive audience. In response to the rise of a literate populace seeking and receiving information through inexpensive newspapers and pamphlets, the government of England sought to restrict the publication of information through what became known as "taxes on knowledge." The November 12, 1830, London *Examiner* carried for the first time on any masthead the following signature: "Paper and Print 3 1/2d. Taxes on Knowledge 3 1/2d." And in 1877 when a marriage manual, *The Fruits of Philosophy*, which had been available for over forty years, was brought out in a cheap six penny edition, its publishers were arrested and tried for obscenity. The defendant, Charles Bradlaugh, argued before Lord Cockburn himself that "it is a horrible thing to put us in danger of imprisonment for giving that information to the poor, which may with impunity be given to the rich" (qtd. in Kendrik 160).

But this "horrible thing" is the very thing that activates censorship. Soon after, the Common Serjeant of the Old Bailey asserted, during England's first obscenity trial of the twentieth century, that a cheaply available book would "clearly tend to the corruption of morals. . . . In the Middle Ages things were discussed which if put forward now before the general public would never be tolerated" (*Regina v. Thompson,* 1900). Characteristically nineteenth century Russian censors would leave George Sands' novels relatively unregulated, but would not tolerate them when they came out in readily affordable editions: "although the censorship has up until now permitted this novel [*Indiana*] with insignificant cuts, it must not be permitted in one of those cheap editions . . . ." *Mauprat* could not be permitted because it "was just reprinted in an illustrated and cheap edition"; and *Le Piccinino* was banned altogether for the reason that the novel was a work "intended for a large mass of readers" (Choldin 50). Similarly, at about the same time during the first half of the nineteenth century in the United States, the "proliferation of state obscenity statutes coincided with an increase in literacy among the American population [and] the beginnings of free universal education . . ." (*Presidential Commission* 353). And in twentieth-century America, the 1934 Motion Picture Code put forth the same reason for censoring motion pictures that the Russian government gave for limiting widespread public access to cheap literary works. Such regulation was justified because motion pictures represented an art that "reaches every class of society," and motion picture "theatres are built for the masses." The "latitude given to film material cannot, in consequence, be as wide as the latitude given to book material." In fact far more latitude is still given to book material, even that consisting of the most cheap sexual content. Thus the members of *The Meese Commission* recognized, in the early 1980's, that "no current prosecution, on the grounds of obscenity, of the printed word occur in the United States, and . . . none are realistically contemplated . . ." (100-1). And in 1996, Wallace and Mangan report that it "is almost universally accepted that the written word . . . is not obscene. Most obscenity prosecutions today involve pictures and films" (33). Also by the end of the century, a bill in Congress, the Communications Decency Act, noting the "extraordinary advance in the availability of . . . informational resources" through the "rapidly developing array of Internet and other interactive computer services" was prepared to censor on the new electronic medium material "available to individual Americans" that, according to Senator Ross Feingold, "would be perfectly legal, and fully protected under the Constitution, in a bookstore or library." In a hearing to determine the constitutionality of the act, Judge Stewart Dalzell seemed troubled by this. "What is it," he wondered, "about this medium--the most democratic of mediums that the human mind has come up with yet--that makes it different from print in terms of the constitutional protection it should receive?"

Judge Dalzell embedded the answer to his question within the question itself. For what makes a work censorable is the people who read or view or are likely to read or view it, and objections to literature, just like those to computer services, are not for its content, but its publicity. It is not the content, but the dissemination of literature that concerns the censor. As the

Williams Report noted, "obscenity is a relative concept. Obscenity proceedings are never against particular material itself and it is always the case . . . that it is the circumstances of publication, particularly in relation to the likely audience, that governs a finding of obscenity, not the content of the material alone" (Bernard Williams 35). So for example "pornography as a regulatory category was invented in response to the perceived menace of the democratization of culture. . . . It was only when print culture opened the possibility of the masses gaining access to writing and pictures that pornography began to emerge as a separate genre of representation" (Hunt 12-3).

Censorship targets not content, but communication. That is why the "tolerance of the community [with respect to objectionable or even otherwise non-objectionable material] may vary according to the medium of representation, even if the content stays the same" (*Regina v. Butler*, 1992, which found such variety of tolerance both justifiable and legitimate). The aim of censorship has always been to limit mass communication, not for the reason often given that the information it presents is inferior to what is intended for a high class audience or that it is immoral or harmful, but because it broadcasts information widely and indiscriminately. So one can usually expect to find renewed calls for censorship with the advent of any novel means of mass communication: print, postal services (for which Anthony Comstock worked), photography, telephones, cinema, radio, audio recordings, television, video recordings, and of late, computer networks.

(Actually almost any new instrument of communication is likely to be attacked. In the 1920's the saxophone, which had been invented but a few decades earlier, was decried as "the devil's flute" whose seductive sounds could drive young girls to a frenzy of uncontrollable passion. In the 1950's rock 'n' roll was said to have the same effect, although those of us who reached puberty in the '50's discovered what our fathers learned in the twenties, that it would take more than music to drive the girls we knew into a frenzy of uncontrollable passion. And when in the '60's we became old enough to buy pornography for ourselves we found that as we approached the *ding-an-sich,* one of the very things we longed to see, lurid pictures of beautiful naked women, that even that could not drive us into a frenzy of uncontrolled passion. Perhaps there was something wrong with us, or the women we knew. Maybe we were being lied to then, as we are now, about the power of the media to drive us all mad. Certainly when it comes to frenzied, uncontrollable passion, religion, war, and soccer seem to have a more potent effect on otherwise ordinarily good and decent folk.)

Censorship as we know it arose in antiquity in response to the spread of written communication itself when it became apparent how significantly that medium differed from oral communication in terms of its social and political consequences. Those who sought to retain exclusive control soon realized that "written communication cannot be monopolized and protected as easily as information that is memorized" (Gauer 184). For example, centralized control of the Chinese people which has lasted up to the present day was first established under the Ch'in dynasty (221-207 B.C.E), but from the beginning men recognized that imperial rule could be maintained only by prohibiting the production and spread of literature. Early on the prime minister, Li Ssu, advised the Emperor of Ch'in on the power of literature to destabilize centralized control and authority: "at present Your Majesty possesses a unified empire, . . . and has firmly established for yourself a position of sole supremacy. And yet these independent schools . . . criticize the codes of laws and instructions. . . . If such license is not prohibited, the sovereign power will decline . . . . Your servant suggests that all books in the imperial archives, save the memoirs of Ch'in, be burned" (*Sources* 154). And thus the Chinese who invented paper were soon to invent the book burning that would accompany it throughout history. Likewise Hinduism, "with its emphasis on stratification and exclusiveness in all aspects of life, not only relied but insisted--more strongly than any other ancient civilization--on the oral transmission of its essentially religious literature" (Gauer 106)

Oral transmission is difficult to censor because it does not broadcast its message in the way written material does, and it perhaps also does not need to be censored for those very reasons. Even a man shouting at the top of his voice cannot be heard very far or for very long: *verba volant, scripta manant* (the spoken word passes, what is written remains). The problem can be handled by simply ostracizing the speaker from the community or giving him hemlock to drink, and no doubt the real reason we no longer execute people for what they say is that in literate culture it is no longer a very effective means of controlling the spread of information. But another reason why oral communication does not pose so great a threat is that it is by its very nature selective and exclusive whereas the nature of written communication is such that it cannot determine its audience.

Thus we find the same pattern of concern with the rise of written communication in Western antiquity: "Writing . . . was an essential element of Greek democracy" (Gaur 156), and the ancients themselves immediately understood its import. Some commentators originally saw the indiscriminate nature of writing as a virtue which would advance open and democratic society, others as a danger which threatened the power of ruling elites, but both recognized it as a significant communications revolution: Legend has it that Phercydes was the first man to put his thoughts into book form and once the book was placed in a library, Galen commended him for his "wise decision to make the book *common property . . . , instead of entrusting it to any particular person . . .* " (Diogenes 45, my italics). And a philosopher like Socrates attacked writing for the same reason that Galen praised it, voicing the identical concern about the nature of literature that Lord Cockburn would express some two thousand years later. He worried that "once a thing is put into writing, the composition . . . drifts all over the place, getting into the hands not only of those who understand it, but equally of those who have no business with it; it doesn't know how to address the right people, and not address the wrong" (*Phaedrus* 159, 158). And what exactly mass media threaten was perhaps first identified most explicitly in a letter Alexander the Great wrote to his tutor, Aristotle. Having heard that Aristotle's lectures had been published he wrote to complain. "You have not done well to publish your books of oral doctrine; *for what is there now that we excel others in, if those things which we have been particularly instructed in be laid open to all?*" Aristotle assured his pupil that his private lessons being both published and unpublished, only men like Alexander who had received oral instruction would be able to understand them (Plutarch 805, my italics). Over the centuries censorship has consistently been justified as a means for protecting the many. But before every man was considered equal either in the eyes of God or under the law, men spoke more openly about the reasons and purpose for controlling and censoring information. Alexander's concern is especially revealing. It tells us that censorship was first recognized rightly as serving to protect the eminence of the few rather than the well-being of the many.

Li Ssu, Socrates and Alexander reacted to the advent of extensive written communication with the same concern censors have shown throughout history whenever a new medium of communication arises which allows information to spread beyond the exclusive control of an elite class to an ever wider audience. The problem then and thereafter had not to do with the information contained within the medium (and that is another reason why censors, try as they might, cannot identify what ought to be illicit on the basis of content). The problem had to do with the potential for the democratization of information, for making what only the few have access to common property indiscriminately available to anyone. The problem then and now has to do with the decentralization of authority and the breakdown of class differences which any medium of mass communication fosters.

Thus censorship as we know it in the modern age is a by-product of the first true medium of mass communication, printing, which made possible (as

Rabelais has Gargantua write to his son, Pantagruel) "such opportunity for studying" that had not been known "in Plato's time." Thanks to the invention of "printed books," thinking was no longer limited to the aristocratic elite as was philosophy in antiquity: "The world is now full of scholarly men, learned teachers, and most ample libraries; indeed I do not think that in the time of Plato, of Cicero, or of Papininian, there were ever so many advantages for study as one may find today. . . . I see brigands, hangmen, freebooters, and grooms nowadays who are more learned than were the doctors and preachers of my time [before printed books]. . . . Why, even the women and the girls have aspired to the credit of sharing this heavenly manna of fine learning" (Book 2, chapter 8). Perhaps a bit of Rabelaisian hyperbole here, yet in 1524 Cardinal Campeggi received a letter from Nurenburg telling the same story: "Every common man is now asking for books or pamphlets and more reading is being done in a day than heretofore in a year" (Putnam II, 287).

And what might very well have been the most successful mass movement in Western history began among the German speaking people as did Guttenberg's printing presses by formulating doctrines that would otherwise have been inconceivable without the mass publication of print literature. For Lutherans took their stand upon the Bible, and such a position would have been impossible were it not for the millions of copies of the Bible which came off the new presses. The central Protestant doctrine of "scriptural sufficiency" could not have been formulated without a sufficient number of reproductions of holy scripture put into circulation among the general population. And the reaction, in terms of edicts seeking to control print publications, quite explicitly state that the problem had to do with the extensive circulation and broad publicity which literary productions were coming to enjoy: As Pope Alexander VI in a 1501 Bull noted, "The art of printing . . . can bring about serious evils if it is permitted to widen the influence of pernicious works" (Putnam I, 80). In 1558 a proclamation of the King and Queen of England seeking to control seditious and heretical expression notes that "divers Books . . . have of late, and dayly be brought into this Realm out of foreign Countries and places beyond the seas, and some also covertly printed within this Realm, and cast abroad in sundry parts thereof . . ." (Putnam I, 91). As Leo XIII later summed the situation up prefatory to publishing the Church's Index of Prohibited Books: "When the invention, in the 15th century, of the new art of printing caused a great increase in the number of books and also a great spread of the pest of evil heresies, it was everywhere deemed necessary to take severe notice of evil writings, both to forestall danger and repair evil already done." The Roman pontiffs had always diligently sought to "prevent the writings of heretics, a constant menace to the community, from making their way unnoticed into circulation" but with the new art of printing, the "great and pernicious influence of wicked writers had more serious and rapid results because of this very increase in the extent of the circulation of literature" (Putnam II, 381-2 & 390). In 1515, two years before Luther published his theses in Wittenburg, Leo X extended church censorship to all writings. By 1542 the Inquisition was empowered by Paul III to do what according to John Milton could not "be heard of, from any ancient state, or polity, or church, nor by any statute left us by our ancestors elder or later; nor from the modern custom of any reformed city, or church abroad." It could prohibit the publication of any book which had not received a licence to be printed. "Till then," Milton contended (wrongly, but no matter), "books were ever as freely admitted into the world as any other birth." The problem was that with the new art of printing, books were being born into the world in such numbers, were multiplying at such a rapid rate as to make prior restraint (the form of censorship Milton specifically objected to) the only practicable means of controlling the birth of these new ideas.

The problem arose again in twentieth-century England with the invention and then the possible open admission into the world of video-cassette recordings, and the government responded in the same way. In 1984 it began licencing video-cassettes to an extent that had not been seen in England since Cromwell's licencing of books and newspapers and soon created the first modern example in Britain of an "Index" of prohibited materials by publishing lists of videos that could not be sold in the United Kingdom.

Those familiar with the never-ending warnings of parents, psychologists, and sociologists about the awful influence television or comic books or movies exercise, how they can so insidiously poison the mind that people will no longer be able to distinguish fact from fantasy or truth from falsehood and may even be driven to act out in real life the fantasies presented by the mass media, these people might be surprised to know that these warnings are by no means new and probably have little or nothing to do with what is being depicted. Responding to the widespread availability of pornography, Catherine MacKinnon, like so many others, has warned that "the consumers want to live out the pornography further in three dimensions. Sooner or later . . . they do. *It* makes them want to; when they believe they can , . . . *they* do" (*Words* 19, MacKinnon's italics, though what they mean to emphasize I cannot figure*)*. But at the beginning of the seventeenth century, one of the world's greatest works of literature was conceived in response to the then new medium of print culture and said pretty much the same thing. Cervantes' masterpiece took those very modern themes about mass media for its subject. His novel was never intended as many think to satirize chivalry, but as it specifically says, when laying out its argument in the beginning, "the entire book is an attack upon *books* of chivalry" (my italics). Alonso Quijana, an otherwise ordinary good and harmless farmer, responds to the new medium of popular print literature in the same way concerned citizens like to tell us the weak and unwary will respond to the material contained in modern media like television soap operas or video pornography. He "became so immersed in his reading that he spent whole nights from sundown to sun up and his days from dawn to dusk in poring over his books, until finally, from . . . so much reading, his brain dried up and he went completely out of his mind" As a result of reading "all sorts of impossible things," he came "to believe that all these fictitious happenings were true; they were more real to him than anything else in the world." All that reading makes Alonso Quijana want to live out what he has read in three dimensions. These days men like Judge Easterbrook tell us that pornography "does not persuade people so much as change them" (*American Book Sellers Ass'n v. Hudnut,* 1985). Three centuries ago Cervantes said the same thing about the popular reading of his day: As a result of reading all the popular fiction of his day, Alonso Quijana changes himself into a knight-errant by the name of Don Quixote de la Mancha.

It does not matter what is being represented, knight erantry or women in bondage, the effect which any medium of mass communication has on ordinarily good people who otherwise have had no previous exposure to what only an elite has read, seen and heard is assumed to be the same: addiction, confusion, poisoning of one's mental faculties, and an overwhelming compulsion to imitate in practice what one has been exposed to in the mass media. In the nineteenth century, reading popular romances drives Emma Bovary into a life of adultery, and it was something of ironic poetic justice that this now classic of modern literature was itself the subject of an obscenity trial based on the very assumption which informed the novel--that, according to the prosecutor, "young girls and, sometimes, married women" who read *Emma Bovary*, could not "withstand the seduction of both senses and feelings" (qtd. in Kendrick 109) and would be made to want to live a life of sin and adultery, would be changed from decent women into adulteresses. In the twentieth century we hear the same thing, that this time young men having read and viewed pornography will be led to "sexually harass their employees and clients, molest their daughters, batter their wives, and use prostitutes . . . gang rape women . . . become serial rapists and sex murderers . . ." (MacKinnon, *Words,* 21). It does not really matter what is being read, since the content of the reading material is not what moves the censor. It is not chivalry but books of chivalry, it is not sexual licence but the licencing and censoring of popular literature and video tapes, that is the concern. Finally of course it is the audience which is targeted: ordinary farmers in the seventeenth century who might fall victim to the mistaken notion that they were true Dons, real knights of the realm. Or poor peasants like Sancho Panza who imagine they might gain a dukedom. Or else the women whom the nineteenth century patriarchs claimed needed protecting by more reasonable men, or the men from whom some twentieth century feminists tell us all women need protection.

There is also one last irony which Cervantes, himself ever the ironist, exploits in the second part of *Don Quixote* which appeared a decade after the publication of the first part. It is that the book which first chronicled the adventures of Don Quixote de la Mancha in order to attack popular fiction became the popular fiction of the day: "Little children leaf through it, young people read it, adults appreciate it, and the aged sing its praises. In short it is so thumbed and read and so well known to persons of every walk in life than no sooner do folks see some skinny nag than they at once cry, 'There goes Rocinante!'" The poor folk in part two who have read the first part begin to mistake ordinary horses for a knight's nag, just as Alonso Quijana in the first part mistook a nag for a knight's stead. That which began as a satire on the confusion popular literature can produce in the minds of its readers becomes responsible for novel confusions among its own readership.

And although Cervantes, undoubtedly feeling a bit different now about popular fiction, ends this self-congratulatory passage with the observation that in *Don Quixote* "there is not to be found an indecent word or a thought that is other than Catholic," the ploy did not work: Perhaps the final irony is that *Don Quixote* which began by attacking books eventually made the Catholic Index of Prohibited Books.

The argument about the seductive power and harmful effects of literature and the like is itself quite seductive and we shall review it in detail in the next section. But as if to show that it is not the insidious content of a medium but the audience it reaches which makes it indecent and deserving of censorship, now that *Don Quixote* and *Madame Bovary* are classics hardly read by persons of every walk in life, but only by college students and literary folk, they no longer concern the censor. In the days when "every common man [was] asking for books" print culture was characterized as aiding "the great spread of the pest of evil." Now that novels are read by an exclusive class of people, the sex and violence found in them does not excite the same concern. But when the themes common to Gothic fiction began appearing in comic books, the warnings of Dr. Federic Wertham about the dangers of comics led to Congressional investigations in the 1950's. At the same time however Wertham was prepared to defend a novel "published by a respected firm." As a witness for the defense he stated that in his opinion "the novel was not obscene and the ban [against it] should be lifted." Under cross-examination he was asked how he could condemn the sexual content of comic books as "having a demoralizing and injurious effect" while testifying that the novel in question was not obscene, to which he answered, in part, that the reason was that the "novel belongs to the realm of literature and art and reaches a relatively small number of readers, while these comic books are mass produced . . . (Wertham 298-9)."

In the 1970's, investigations and calls for censorship occurred when depictions of sex and violence began to appear in a video format and again in the '80's when their presence in rock music became noticeable. And in 1957 those who could pay top dollar to see the new musical, *West Side Story*, could hear with perhaps some shock but with no restraints, that the Jets could "beat every last fuckin' gang on the whole fuckin' street." That wording did not find its way into the generally more affordable movie version.

The argument given by censors, like those who sat on the Meese Commission, is that regulation is needed because the nature of something like pornography had changed since a previous Presidential Commission had declared it harmless. It is the argument frequently offered--that some novelty of foulness demands control. But pornography in 1980 was no different from 1970 except that video tapes for one had made under-the-counter material previously available only to the few who sought it out in some urban centers like New York or Los Angeles readily available to anyone, anywhere in the United States who owned a VCR and could afford the postage and handling charges.

In 1985, Tottie Ellis called for censorship by noting, "Twenty years ago pornography was hard to find. Today [in movies, magazines, network and cable television] it is difficult to avoid"(*USA Today*, May 1, 1985). Nor were there any new heresies in the 15th century when Gutenberg came out with his printing press, certainly none created by the medium. The human animal has not evolved during the entire but relatively short period that human culture has existed on the planet. Our desire for pleasure, and the variety of forms it takes, our compulsion to cruelty and violence has not changed one bit since the dawn of human history and it will not change until some genetic mutation over millions and millions of years serves to alter our species. There are no novel perversions, no new evils which culture creates. What changes culture has wrought throughout history is the ever increasing availability of information to more and more classes of people which has led not to the massive corruption censors bewail, but to the elimination of exclusive control. With the onset of *glasnost* in Soviet Russia, "all of a sudden, what only the ruling elite and its lackeys had been able to enjoy at closed viewing sessions was becoming accessible to all. The end of the world was nigh!" (Kon, 115). Indeed censors are right to warn about the end of the world, for new media of mass communication have proven over and again to spell the end of one world and the beginning of another, and those who seek to preserve the advantages they posses will censor every new form of communication as a means of keeping their world and the privileges they enjoy in it from ending.

Chapter 4

The Question of Harm
and the Evidence for It

That certain expression needs to be prohibited because of the harm it causes remains for many the censors most powerful and compelling argument. But it is also the most bogus claim he or she makes! It has never stood up to serious scrutiny because 1) people, including those otherwise opposed to censorship, are not naive and do recognize the need to control information when there is a clear and present danger of real harm or damage, however 2) no reliable evidence exists that the expression censors usually seek to suppress actually causes harm, and so 3) censors who claim harm are either making assertions without supporting evidence or ignoring contradictory evidence, or else 4) having no reasonable explanation or physical evidence for the harms they claim, they depend upon the discredited belief in the power of black magic and demon possession--the idea which the censor knowingly or unwittingly puts forth that through contact with certain forms of expression individuals and entire societies can become possessed of various disorders and pathologies, and finally and most significantly 5) modern censorship rulings, fully aware of the problem censors have presenting convincing evidence of any actual damage expression can cause, have regularly taken these difficulties into account and have decided over and again that proof of actual harm will not be required to censor expression as a criminal offence!

When considering the issue of harm it might be helpful to begin by differentiating between suppression of *information* and censorship of *ideas*. There is usually comparatively little or no objection to the suppression of vital information in times of war or peace because most people recognize that real harm or damage may occur if and when information gets into the wrong hands. They understand that information respecting troop movements, battle plans, weapons development and the like cannot be allowed to fall into enemy hands and that trade or government secrets can justifiably be kept from competitors or adversaries. This is not to say that there is no reason for concern over the suppression of information: business, political or religious institutions may attempt to suppress damaging information regarding corrupt, immoral or illegal activities; the claim of national security is often a smokescreen governments use to protect not the nation but the party in power; and scientific work is severely hindered if not made impossible without the free exchange of information.

So long as we are noting differences we might also observe that perhaps another reason why there is not so serious objection to the suppression of information is that it tends to target persons different from those who are subject to the censorship of opinions and beliefs. With respect to information, the concern is that it might fall into the hands of enemies or competitors. Thus it mattered tremendously in the early 1940's what some German or Japanese citizens might know about American research into atomic energy or in the 1980's about research in superconductivity. During times of war or peace, Americans try to keep vital information from the Japanese or the Russians, and General Motors from Chrysler or Ford. However, when it comes to matters of moral, religious, or political opinions, the concern is not with the foreigner, since it does not usually matter to a Protestant in Philadelphia what a Shintoist in Kyoto believes or says about religion. The concern when it comes to moral, religious or political opinions is with the perceived "outsider" within the group who gives expression to "heretical" or "alien and seditious" ideas. In these matters, Catholics censor Catholics, Shintoists do it to Shintoists, and Frenchman to the citizens of France. As a result, censorship of opinions, coming as it does from the government under which, or the community within which one lives, affects numerous aspects of the lives of ordinary citizens--how they think, what they can say or read, or how they can behave--to an extent that the suppression of information never does. Furthermore, when we seek to withhold information from outsiders it is because we assume them to be just as clever as we. Propaganda often paints them as exceedingly and even ruthlessly clever. But as we have seen, censoring opinions works on the opposite assumption, that certain members within our own society possess a diminished moral and intellectual capacity.

I will propose in the next section reasons why most all censorship has historically been concerned with moral, religious and political opinions and not usually matters of fact. For our present purpose we need only note that most all people are not the gullible fools censors often take them to be when it comes to the issue of serious danger. When confronted with the possibility of a clear and present danger they need little convincing and readily understand the need for secrecy and censorship, but many remain unconvinced when confronted with modern claims of harmful expression for the simple reason that they recognize that the claim in these cases has little or no justification.

Still and all, because censors, especially these days, seem always to be talking about harm and because the assumption that obscene material causes harm is widespread, one of the most significant misunderstandings people have is their belief that harm is the issue which favors censors and which their opponents therefore wish everyone would ignore. Nothing could be further from the truth. Contrary to what many believe and what some would have us believe, the dismissal rather than the consideration of the question of harm remains to this day the most crucial aspect of censorship in modern democracies. *It is in fact the censors and not their opponents who have traditionally sought to dismiss the question of harm from consideration.* And the law has regularly accommodated them in their need.

As we shall see, the modern Anglo-American tradition of censorship, which first began to treat offensive expression as a punishable *secular* crime, began in eighteenth-century England when the courts ruled that evidence of actual harm would not be required to convict persons for obscene expression or indecent behavior. And censorship in contemporary society, operating in accordance with the very same legal precedents that were first established close to three hundred years ago, has survived to this very day precisely because censors still manage to rebuff attempts to make harm a significant and determining factor in deciding upon the legality of expression. Thus when *The Presidential Commission on Pornography and Obscenity* challenged obscenity law because it could find no evidence that "exposure to or use of explicit sexual materials play a significant role in the causation of social or individual harms," Charles Keating, Jr., newly appointed to the Commission by President Nixon, quickly pointed out that "the reasons for obscenity laws are *not* contained in the statement [of the Commission regarding harm]. Obscenity laws have existed historically in recognition of the need to protect the *public morality*" *(*617*).* As we shall see, Keating was correct. The history of obscenity law indeed did not turn on the issue of harm, and Keating, founder of Citizens for Decent Literature, did not wish to have the law reformed so that it would. Nor did his counterparts in England who were the first to move, as one feminist critic put it, "to jettison 'effects theories' as unhelpful to the case for censorship": In 1986 England's Parliament debated a bill to extend the Obscene Publications Act to television, and Tory MP Douglas Hogg, for one, admitted that "a causal connection between violence on television and the commission of violent offences . . . has not been clearly established. [However] society is entitled to say that certain matters are so offensive that they should not be published, even if we cannot establish that they have a prejudicial effect" (qtd. in Merck 192). In 1992 the Canadian Supreme Court noted that "civil liberty groups . . . concede that harm can justify state intervention, but they deny that any harm flows from obscene materials . . . ," however in defending the Court's support for the obscenity code, it was held that in order to proscribe obscene material "scientific proof is not required, and reason and common experience will often suffice" (*Regina v. Butler*). And we might finally recall and complete Mary Whitehouse's remarks to the 1987 Conservative Party Conference: "you've got to get away from this silly business of having to prove things. We've got to start using our common sense and human experience, then we might get somewhere."

Contemporary censors recognize that "having to prove things" undermines their whole endeavor. It introduces a radical change in a branch of law which has historically succeeded in convicting men and women for centuries on the basis not of objective evidence, but upon what common sense already *believes* to be true. We will soon find this position stated over and over again by those seeking to censor, that harm is not the issue and that the lack of evidence demonstrating any significant correlation expression has to harm is therefore irrelevant, since proof of harm is not required in order to censor objectionable material, and that, finally, in lieu of actual evidence, judges and juries may legitimately defer to conventional folk wisdom, to the common sense supposition that certain kinds of expression, even if the thing can't be proven to cause actual harm, must cause harm of some kind or other.

In a recent article (*London Sunday Times,* March 31, 1996), Bryan Appelyard lamented that video and film censorship wasn't working. He cited Mill's famous statement that the only reason civilized society has for exercising power over any of its members "is to prevent harm to others," but then he typically went on to comment, "It sounds reasonable enough, . . . a clear guide for action. Except that, now, harm is everywhere, dispersed throughout society, seeping into our heads, drifting through unfathomable surroundings. Something seems wrong, something seems harmful, but we don't know what it is."

The sequence of Appelyard's thoughts reveal in a nutshell the kinds of difficulties we will find censors having to confront and the kinds of "solutions" we will find them resorting to. First off, Appelyard recognizes that many people in modern liberal democracies accept as a clear guide to action that citizens can be restrained only to prevent harm to others.

Appleyard finds that reasonable enough--at least he says it sounds reasonable. What one might expect to follow from this is the statement that obscenity does/does not cause harm and therefore should/should not be censored. But Appleyard avoids the question of actual harm--no doubt because, I think we can fairly assume, having no evidence for it he would therefore have to reject the need for controls on the grounds that obscenity presents no proven danger to society. So he quickly skips over that silly business of having to prove things and diverts attention away from verifiable assertions about real harm. But having done that, all he is left to argue for is the vague sense which many people have that "something seems wrong," that some unfathomable "harm" is being done to our heads, even though "we don't know what it is."

There is nothing unfathomable about actual harm, and no one could say that they don't know or could not find out what that is. But would-be censors regularly seem to show no interest in such identifiable dangers and ignore, skip over, or dismiss the question of actual evidence of real harm in favor of common sense notions based upon vague intuitions of unfathomable things. And why not? After all, at any time anyone can count on the fact that large segments of any population feel that something is wrong. Knowing what the causes are can prove to be a difficult if not impossible task, far more difficult than appealing to commonly held beliefs and prejudices and then raiding a few bookshops to put people's minds at rest that the police are getting at the root of the problem. When all is said and done it is a lot less risky, both in terms of community reaction and potential for gunfire, to protect the citizenry by confiscating dirty books than deadly weapons. (The gay movement had its Stonewall, but I have yet to hear of the patrons and proprietors of an adult bookstore fighting back a police raid. In America, homosexuals in New York, Branch Davidians in Waco, Texas, or Survivalist in Montana have more gumption--and maybe more open support--than the tens of thousands of law-abiding citizens across the country who would just like to look at a dirty book in peace.)

The primary point I wish the reader to keep in mind in upcoming discussion is not that there exists little or no reliable evidence for harm. There in fact doesn't, but my approach to the question will not be primarily to search out evidence of harm, but to analyze the claims of those who view and would have the rest of us view expression as causing harm. From them we will discover two revealing problems:

The first is that sooner or later they themselves repeatedly and consistently admit that there exists no reliable evidence for the claims they make. This strikes me as the quickest and arguably the surest way to show absence of reliable evidence, and that is how I hope to do it. So even though I will not be extensively reviewing and analyzing studies, I do not ask the reader to take my word for it, if and when I say there is no such evidence. I ask her or him to take the word of those who claim harm and who in many cases have reviewed the evidence. If they, by their own admission, cannot find convincing evidence of actual harm and do not present any, that is pretty convincing evidence that no such evidence exists.

The second thing we will find is that those who speak of harm, because they are unable to find reliable evidence for such a claim, finally dismiss the need for scientific or other supporting evidence in order to institute the legal constraints they call for. Their position, often stated quite explicitly and written into numerous statutes, is that to merely assume, or believe, or assert that some expression is harmful is sufficient reason to censor it regardless of the evidence or lack of evidence.

I have found that there is indeed good evidence that there exists little good evidence of harm, and it is best found in those who claim harm. On the basis of extensive research done by myself and others I think we can safely say that there is not now and never has been evidence of expression causing actual harm. However, lest the reader think I am ultimately avoiding the issue, a quick review of some recent findings will suggest the kind of evidence censors chose to ignore or dismiss.

After a survey of researches all over the world, the Council states 'that, as far as the Council is aware, no scientific experiments exist which can lay a basis for the assumption that pornography or "obscene" pictures and films contribute to the committing of sexual offences by normal adults or young people. On the basis of psychiatric and child-psychiatric experience it can neither be assumed that sexual leanings, the development of personality, and the ordinary attitude to sex and ethical-sexual norms either in children or adults, can be detrimentally affected by the means in question (pornographic literature, pictures and films). . . . This statement holds good regardless of whether the pornographic writings, pictures, etc. are of normal or sexually perverted content.

[The] case against obscenity rests, ultimately . . . , not upon any hard factual analysis of any anti-social consequences. (*Report of the Arts Council of Great Britain*, 1962)

In sum, empirical research, designed to clarify the question, has found no evidence to date that exposure to explicit sexual materials plays a significant role in the causation of delinquent or criminal behavior among youth or adults, . . . sexual or nonsexual deviancy or severe emotional disturbances. (*Presidential Commission on Obscenity and Pornography*, 1970)

[W]e unhesitatingly reject the suggestion that the available statistical information for England and Wales lends any support at all to the argument that pornography acts as a stimulus to the commission of sexual violence" (*Committee on Obscenity and Film Censorship, 1979*).

Experiments [correlating viewing violent and sexist material with violent and abusive behavior towards women] that have done follow up studies have almost invariably shown that there is little or no long-term effect of the laboratory experiments on the men's behavior. . . . [W]e need to be quite clear that there is little *scientific* evidence [for the argument that such material causes violent and abusive behavior]. (Julienne Dickey & Gail Chester, *Feminism and Censorship, 1988)*

Correlational studies in this country [the United States], Europe, and Asia, find *no* rise in sexual violence with the availability of sexual material. No reputable research shows a causal link between obscenity and violence. (Ad Hoc Committee of Feminists for Free Expression, 1992).

When the Michelson-Morley experiment demonstrated that the ether did not exist, everyone did not keep insisting that it did exist and that we had a right to assume it existed and should keep on looking for it. People were not upset by the loss of the ether as they were by the loss of a geocentric universe because the ether was never the subject of theology or our common sense of our own worth. Now admittedly the social sciences are not as exact as the so-called "hard" sciences like physics (actually the hard sciences are not so exact as most people think). Nevertheless the methodology of the social sciences, consisting of clinical experiments, interviews, surveys, and statistical analysis, has been with us for generations and one can't reasonably suspect that they are so primitive as to have consistently arrived at the very same wrong conclusion over and over again. Decade after decade they have shown what a minority have known and argued for, that there is no evidence for the assumption that obscenity causes harm to individuals or society. The proof is in, and reasonable people will have to abandon their faith in the evils of obscenity just as reasonable people have given up the belief that the earth is flat and does not move. If decade after decade people continue to assert what has been demonstrated to be unfounded, responsible individuals cannot and must not accept their assertions as reasonable nor tolerate their campaigns as just.

If history has a purpose, Nietzsche quipped, we would have found it already. In the latter half of the twentieth century there has hardly been any subject more systematically studied than the relationship of obscenity to anti-social behavior, crime and delinquency. If obscenity produces harm, we can now assuredly say, we would have found it already. But we haven't, and we can safely say that there is none. The reason we have been blessed with so many studies on the subject is, no doubt, the same reason why we have so many studies on the effects of the birth control pill or clinical abortions on the patient, or why we have so many doubts being bandied about concerning the theory of evolutionary biology. It is not that the experiments and follow-up studies were ill-conceived, their methodology faulty or the conclusions inappropriate to the evidence. It is that the procedures and conclusions offend traditional morality. The evidence that obscene material is not harmful is solid. There is today no reason to question that evidence other than the fact that some people simply don't like the conclusion.

One more point by way of introducing the subject. I expect that many do sympathize with the general view that science, particularly the social sciences which do study these questions, are faulty and limited and are still and all not the only way to arrive at the truth. Many more may feel that I place too much confidence in these studies or make too much of the fact that the censors dismiss them. Perhaps they do or will feel that, as the censors keep saying, we need to defer instead to human experience and common sense. But I think we will see that the censors finally reject not only empirical science but observations of any kind. I for one would love to see human experience and common sense truly come into play when judging their claims. For I think we will see that the things they say really happen are really fictions of their own devising. If we would pause and think for a moment, we would recognize that people exposed to indecent literature and obscene expression simply do not experience the things censors say they do, and if we would truly and honestly use our common sense when listening to their claims we would recognize that they are quite obviously ridiculous-- they violate everything we know about how we are constituted, about how we react and behave with respect to the things we hear and read, and about the power which oral and written communication clearly does *not* have over our lives.

In 1573 the Council of Trent permitted the publication of Boccaccio's *Decameron* on condition that the sexual sins it described were changed to be committed by lay people and not, as originally written, by nuns and priests. European societies typically sought to suppress as profane or libelous expression critical of religion or politics, but it was not until the rise of the middle class in modern times that they sought to regulate expression depicting bodily functions. English common law did not recognize obscenity or indecency as a criminal offence until the eighteenth century, and when it did, the matter turned upon the issue of harm: *In order to make indecency a criminal offence, the courts agreed that harm could be said to occur without presenting any evidence of physical force or damage.*

In 1707 an unsuccessful attempt was made to criminalize obscenity as a common law offence. James Read was brought up on a charge of obscenity before the Queen's Bench for publishing *The Fifteen Plagues of the Maiden Head.* Read contended that the publication constituted no crime under English common law and chief Justice John Holt agreed, "If we have no precedent we cannot punish. Shew me a precedent." The crown offered the 1663 conviction of Sir Charles Sedley for public indecency, as he had stood naked and drunk upon a balcony, but Justice John Powell disagreed:

> This [case against Mr. Read] is for printing bawdy stuff, but reflects on no person or persons or against the Government [i.e., it is not libelous] . . . . If there is no remedy in the Spiritual court, it does not follow that there must be a remedy here. There is no law to punish it. I wish there were . . . . It indeed tends to the corruption of good manners, but that is not sufficient for us to punish. As to the case of sir Charles Sedley, there was something more in that case than shewing his naked body in the balcony; for that case was quod vi et armis [with force and violence] he pissed down upon people's heads. (qtd. in Levy 306)

In those days criminal law dealt with conduct that caused injury of some kind, as was the case with Sir Sedley whose offence under common law was not, as the crown tried to claim, public indecency, but actions involving force and violence against other persons. The judges agreed that the secular courts could not punish behavior simply because some found it to be ill-mannered. *At the beginning of the eighteenth century, there was no English law which allowed for the punishment of bawdiness, public indecency, or the corruption of good manners in the criminal courts!* This was the opinion not only of a justice of the Queen's bench, but of one who wished for such laws. He didn't have long to wait. For with the rise to power of the Puritan middle class in the late seventeenth and early eighteenth century, offences to moral decency became a criminal matter and the chief reason for regulating and prosecuting expression as obscene. Justice Powell has gotten his wish. From the eighteenth century to the present day there has been no end to criminal statutes regulating morals and manners.

The criminalization of indecency and obscenity required three sweeping changes: First, good or bad manners had to be elevated to an issue of moral concern. Secondly, morals offences themselves had to be reinterpreted as something which it was the duty of the temporal power to guard against and punish. Thirdly, the criminalization of bawdy and ill-mannered behavior and expression required a redefinition of harm. All of this was set in motion in what Chief Justice Robert Raymond called "a case of very great consequence." In 1728 Edmund Curll was charged with obscenity before the King's Bench. He had been convicted and released in 1725, once again on the grounds that only the ecclesiastical courts had jurisdiction in such matters. Histories of the subject usually cite the 1663 Sedley conviction as initiating obscenity law as a modern secular offence, and clearly men of the time wanted to give it great importance. However, as late as 1725 they were being rebuked in the courts.

There is no question of the importance of the Sedley conviction, but not as a precedent-setting case. Justices, like John Holt, did not accept it as a precedent setting-cases simply because Sedley's criminal conviction resulted from his using force and violence against persons, and there was nothing new in that. Without force and violence that injures persons, bawdy behavior in and of itself was not cause for criminal conviction. What was needed was a case in which injury to persons could be said to occur without the use of force and violence. Over and over again in modern society we hear from church leaders, judges, or anti-porn feminists that obscene literature is in and of itself harmful and subject to prosecution. The injury it does to persons is said to be overwhelming. Yet throughout all these warnings and prohibitions, there is never evidence presented and finally none needed to demonstrate the existence of these various harms. Why? Because ever since the *Curll* ruling it was decided that bawdy behavior and expression could injure persons without the use of actual force! *Practically all censorship in modern society depends upon this presumption, that criminal injury can occur without the use of actual force!*

Thus the precedent setting case of great consequence for most all modern censorship efforts and rulings has been the 1728 conviction of Edmund Curll, and its precedent-setting significance was the way in which it redefined the question of force and injury. After repeated failures by the crown to gain criminal conviction for obscenity, the Attorney General of England himself now argued for the criminalization of obscenity under common law: "this is an offence at common law as it tends to corrupt the morals of the King's subjects and is against the peace of the King. Peace includes good order and government and that *peace may be broken in many instances without an actual force* . . ."[my italics]. The Attorney General cited conduct "against morality" as an example of breaking the peace without force, and argued that an "immoral act . . .if it is destructive of morality in general . . . is an offence of a publick nature." And this time the court agreed, holding that insofar as religion was part of common law "therefore whatever is an offence against that, is evidently an offence against the common law. Now morality is the fundamental part of religion, and therefore whatever strikes against that must for the same reason be an offence against the common law."

In this way, modern bourgeois society sought to recover in a secularized form the church-state alliance which had begun to break down with the Reformation. With the decline of the power of the ecclesiastical courts in the seventeenth century, there was no power to punish sin, including those sinful ideas involving heresy, blasphemy and atheism. Ecclesiastical power, and the institutions that enforced it, was justified because it sought to save souls from damnation. That was not a state concern, especially once Protestantism began to draw a sharp line between church and state. The modern, particularly Protestant state clearly needed to find some other justification for punishing beliefs, particularly since Protestants contended that religious belief was not a state concern: "a false Religion and Worship will not hurt the Civill State," Roger Williams remarked, "in case the worshipers breake no civill Law: the civill lawes not being broken, civill Peace is not broken . . ."(198). It is just these kinds of sentiments which the Attorney General of England attacked when he successfully argued before the King's Bench that the civil law had an interest in ideas because they possessed the power to break the civil peace without an actual force.

Thus the modern state argued that certain ideas, attitudes, and feelings fell under the jurisdiction of the criminal law, not because they were sinful (sin was a matter between God and the individual conscience), but because even though physical force was not in evidence they were in fact harmful (and thus a concern to everyone). Thus in the 1992 decision of the Canadian Supreme Court to outlaw pornography (the *Butler* decision we will review shortly), the Court went to great lengths to insist that though it sought to censor obscene material on the assumption that it encouraged certain attitudes and beliefs, its objection to those attitudes and beliefs was not that they offended morality per se, but that they could be presumed without proof to pose a potential threat to society.

Hebrew scriptures emphasized right and wrong in terms of actions, and they present us with 613 commandments and prohibitions concerned almost exclusively with how one should or should not act. Christianity from the first insisted that one was accountable and would be judged perhaps above all on the basis of what one thought and felt. In the West the power of thought and feeling to save or damn is a legacy of Christianity. (Indeed the innermost thoughts of individuals was originally of so little concern that except for those thoughts which lead immediately to significant action, it would be impossible to determine from the literature what Achilles, or Moses, or Samson thought in the privacy of their own minds.) So when in the seventeenth century secular institutions inherited from the ecclesiastical courts the power to punish ideas, they ascribed to ideas, attitudes, and feelings the same power to injure, harm or destroy: ideas were still regarded as they always had been as having the power to corrupt souls, but now corruption and depravity was a matter of state because corrupt individuals or groups of individuals were said to pose a threat to the fundamental values of society at large.

Protestantism had called for the inviolability of the individual conscience in spiritual matters, and thus for freedom of religious opinion. The principle, central to modern liberal thought, that overt acts alone are punishable and that there should exist, in Jefferson's words, "a complete wall of separation between church and state" originated as religious doctrine. Protestantism went a long way towards freeing individuals and societies of believers from state interference, and it did so not simply as a matter of religious principle, but as a means of preventing bloodshed and securing peace within secular society. Secular authority, one anonymous author argued in Nuerenburg in 1530, "should use its sceptre or sword . . . against external misdeeds, so that no one may be harmed in his body or goods. . . . [I]t is neither right nor possible for the secular government, by means of its sceptre of the sword, to give anyone true faith or the holy spirit, [and] it is neither right nor possible to drive out false faith, heresy, or the devil by means of the sword" (Estes 45). In 1664 Roger Williams wrote in his *The Bloudy Tenant of Persecution*: "All civil states, with their officers of justice . . . [are] essentially civil, and therefore not judges, governors, defenders of the spiritual, or Christian, state and worship. . . . God requires not an uniformity of religion to be enacted and enforced in any civil state, which uniformity, sooner or later, is the cause of civil war. . . "(3) .

Maurice Girodios has contended that all "our political structures are directly inherited from the theocratic model of antiquity, reinforced and modernized by the Roman Caesars, and again reinforced in the middle ages by the technological alliance of Church and State ("Preface" *Obscenity Report*, 23). But by the time of the Reformation, one very significant and influential aspect of Protestantism presented a serious challenge to those theocratic structures modeled upon Church-State alliance. It challenged the control which ecclesiastical institutions had over the conscience of the believer. The heritage of theocratic rule had been seriously threatened, but was ultimately maintained by virtue of the fact that the emerging secular state responded to the challenge of Protestantism by appropriating that ecclesiastical power unto itself. To understand modern obscenity law, its roots and aims, we have to understand the history of blasphemy and heresy, which is just what American Constitutional scholar, Leonard Levy did in two excellent studies: *Treason Against God* and *Blasphemy*. Practically all obscenity law in modern, so-called secular society derives from and continues to enforce the ancient concerns of organized, state religions. For as Levy notes, "one of the most important developments in the history of the law of blasphemy" was that the "law of obscenity derived from the doctrine that religion, Christianity in particular, is part of the common law of the land" (*Blasphemy* 304-5). Indeed we might go so far as to say that censorship itself represents the clearest continuing manifestation of Church-State alliance in modern society, and no society that censors as ours do can claim to be a truly secular one wherein its citizens remain free from unwelcome religious interference by government in the conduct of their lives.

In the end so long as the modern state granted religious freedom with regard to spiritual matters, as exemplified in the First Amendment to the U.S. Constitution, Protestants and others were pretty much unperturbed by the fact that it retained theocratic control and continued to interfere in many other matters of conscience. Secure in the right to their own religious beliefs, Protestants and others hardly protested when the modern state made matters of conscience a secular concern punishable under criminal law in the temporal courts: How many times have Americans heard that freedom of expression is limited, that the government retains a right to proscribe it, and how many times has it done so? On the other hand how many times do we hear that freedom of religion is limited, that the government has a right to restrain it, and how many times has it done that? Most Supreme Court decisions regarding religion have had to do with the "establishment" and not the "free exercise" clause of the First Amendment and seek to maintain a separation of church and state, rather than limit the free exercise of religion. (Keeping government out of religion is not part of any atheistic plot as many on the religious right claim today. Rather, as the founding fathers understood when drafting the Constitution, it remains a necessity for the free exercise of religion in the United States. "The experience of the United States," James Madison wrote in 1821, "is a happy disproof of the error . . . that without a legal incorporation of religious and civil polity, neither could be supported. A mutual independence is found most friendly to practical Religion, to social harmony, and to political prosperity." Earlier the man who is often called the father of the Constitution noted that the "number, the industry, and the morality of the Priesthood, & the devotion of the people have been manifestly increased by the total separation of the Church from the State" [see respectively his letters to Schaeffer, Dec. 3, 1821 & to Walsh, March 2, 1819]. Nor was Madison's enthusiasm limited to the prosperity of Christian sects only, as evidenced by his letters of May 15, 1818 and August 1820 expressing the same sentiments to two Jewish correspondents. And more than two hundred years after the Constitution was written and ratified studies continue to show that religious devotion in the United States continues to be higher than in almost any other country surveyed.)

Thus it was left to the modern liberal tradition to extend the freedoms the Reformation called for in spiritual matters to the secular state itself and to continue the challenge to theocratic rule in modern times. It reacted against efforts to criminalize in secular society what religion had already left to the individual conscience within the society of believers. In the late eighteenth century Jefferson for example complained, "The error seems not sufficiently eradicated that the operations of the mind, as well as the acts of the body, are subject to the coercion of the laws. . . . *The legitimate powers of government extend to such acts only as are injurious to others.* But it does me no injury for my neighbor to say that there are twenty gods, or no God. It neither picks my pocket nor breaks my leg" (Dumbauld 36, my italics). By the nineteenth century the bourgeois propensity for penalizing harmless conduct had become so much a part of modern law and society that the classic work of modern liberalism was composed "to assert one very simple principle" in reaction to it. The object of *On Liberty,* Mill wrote, was to assert the principle that "the sole end for which mankind are warranted . . . in interfering with the liberty of action of any of their number, is self-protection. That the only purpose for which power can be rightfully exercised over any member of a civilized community, against his will, is to prevent harm to others."

Many have tried to make a supposedly ignorant public aware of the harms they contend obscene and indecent expression cause and which they accuse liberal-minded people of refusing to recognize and therefore helping to contribute to. Yet the fact of the matter is that the opponents of censorship and repression have not deliberately closed their eyes to the matter of harm. It is not censors, but writers like Jefferson and Mill whom we find insisting that crime and punishment must rest upon the question of harm. Indeed their opinions were formulated in response to the censors themselves who had in fact sought and succeeded in eliminating harm as a consideration when determining the legal status of expression. If proof of harm were required to suppress expression, then most obscenity cases over the past few centuries would have been thrown out for lack of evidence. For it is precisely because obscenity cases were being dismissed in the temporal courts for the absence of any evidence of harm that prosecutors in the eighteenth century sought and succeeded in making obscenity a secular offence by voiding the issue of harm altogether in such cases, and for approximately three hundred years now the courts have repeatedly ruled that offensiveness in and of itself constitutes the crime of obscenity *without regard to the question of harm.*

The first time the question of obscenity was squarely put to the U. S. Supreme Court (*Roth vs. The United States,* 1957*),* Justice Brennan, writing for the majority and recognizing the historical connection with religious concerns--he noted that "profanity and obscenity were related offences"--observed that obscenity was not a matter of actual harm, but of speech and behavior that tended to offend "the social interest in order and morality." In keeping with the legal tradition established in eighteenth-century England and the even longer tradition regarding blasphemy from which the secular crime of obscenity derived, the Court ruled that "convictions may be had without proof either that obscene material will perceptibly create a clear and present danger of antisocial conduct, or will probably induce its recipients to such conduct." It was no offence against the constitutional guarantee of free speech that courts "punish incitation to impure sexual thoughts, not shown to be related to any overt antisocial conduct." And when the Supreme Court of Canada outlawed pornography thirty-five years later, it entertained the idea that "proof of actual harm should be required," but concluded that outlawing pornography "does not demand actual proof of harm" (*Butler v. The Queen,* 1992*).*

The views of Andrea Dworkin and Catherine MacKinnon greatly influenced the *Butler* decision, and in *Only Words* MacKinnon praises it at length as an exemplary pornography ruling. In the very same book she writes, "What is wrong with pornography is that it hurts women . . . . What is wrong with obscenity law is that this reality has no role in it" (88*).* But there is nothing new in the *Butler* decision that her views helped fashion, since actual hurt to women finally plays no part in its fundamental assumptions. *Butler* would indeed have presented a new and different approach had it demanded proof of actual harm as a necessary precondition for censoring pornographic material. In not doing so *Butler* merely reiterated the logic and the standard that have guided obscenity rulings for close to three centuries. It ultimately states that whatever the reality or unreality of actual harm, whether pornography really and truly hurts women or anyone else or does no harm whatsoever, no proof of such harm shall be required in order to censor it--one does not have "to prove things," one need only presume them.

One paragraph early on in the majority ruling shows how the thinking merely repeats that of the 1728 *Curll* decision:

> The overriding objective of s[ection] 163 [of the criminal code which deals with obscenity] is not moral disapprobation but the avoidance of harm to society. The proliferation of materials which seriously offend the values fundamental to our society is a substantial concern which justifies restricting the otherwise full exercise of freedom of expression. . . . While a direct link between obscenity and harm to society may be difficult, if not impossible, to establish, it is reasonable to presume that exposure to images bears a causal relationship to changes in attitudes and beliefs. There is a sufficiently rational link between the criminal sanction, which demonstrates the community's disapproval of the dissemination of materials which potentially victimize women and which restricts the negative influences which such materials have on changes in attitudes and behavior, and the objective [of avoidance of harm to society].

Notice how as the evidence for *actual* harm becomes admittedly difficult if not impossible to establish, the justification shifts to restrictions placed upon certain materials which are said to influence not actions directly, but attitudes and beliefs which may be presumed to cause *potential* harm. Now there is equally no evidence cited to prove that images bear a causal relationship to negative changes in attitudes and beliefs, any more than there is evidence presented that images bear a causal relationship to negative attitudes. But juries may presume that such a causal relationship exists, and the court would allow that such a presumption would be "reasonable." Once that presumption is permitted and in place, presumptuousness is upgraded to what is described as "a sufficiently rational link" connecting obscene materials which may be presumed to negatively affect attitudes and beliefs, to attitudes and beliefs which may be understood to have the potential to harm women, to the actual harms women have been known to suffer, and thus we may finally throw out all the middle terms and conclude that obscene material may be restricted with the objective of avoiding harm to society. Lacking empirical evidence that obscene material actually harms women, the court will permit that a connection founded upon a presumption would be sufficiently rational to restrict obscene material.

Carole Vance has noted how censors currently disguise their old-fashioned concerns about sexual sin and immorality by taking a public stance against violence (see below). *Butler* also insists early on that it censors out of a felt need to avoid harm to society and women in particular. But look at how it defines harm. No sooner does the court claim that its objective is "not moral disapprobation," than it defines harm as that which might "offend the values fundamental to our society." No causal link can be established between obscenity and actual harm, so in view of that difficulty, harm is quickly redefined as that which may occur, in the words of *Curll* (1728) "without an actual force" striking "against morality."

To demand such proof of the reality of harm as a pre-requisite for censoring obscenity would put a burden of proof upon the would-be censor which she does not wish to bear. If censors truly and confidently believe that there is reliable evidence that pornography hurts women and that obscenity law is wrong for not considering evidence of the harm it does, then I would think they might find good reason to question the logic of rulings like *Butler*. On the other hand, if anyone might wish to stigmatize pornography, along with its producers, performers and consumers by crying over and again that it harms women without presenting convincing proof to substantiate their charges, then the wording of the *Butler* decision, and that of just about every other obscenity ruling, addresses their position perfectly and remains the most suitable and favorable wording they can hope for.

It may very well be that pornography affects attitudes and beliefs, but I can think of a whole range of attitudes and beliefs which it affects that correlate with a society that has in many respects grown more, not less tolerant and hateful as pornography has become more widely available to men and women as well: the recognition without condemnation of female sexuality, the recognition and acceptance of different lifestyles, again especially when it comes to women, the knowledge of a greater range of sexual techniques and practices beyond intercourse in the missionary position, the adoption of those practices by men to provide themselves and their female partners with greater fulfillment, the realization that human beings may find pleasure and fulfillment with partners of their own sex, the recognition by sexual minorities that they are not alone and not sick and immoral, etc., etc. But at least in the United States, we cannot argue that pornography is not speech or expression, just an aid to masturbation (MacKinnon) or violence in and of itself (Itzin), and therefore not deserving of First Amendment protection which speech has, and then say that it ought to be censored because it adversely affects attitudes towards women (or anyone else).

Finally, MacKinon's contention that obscenity law is wrong for not considering the hurt pornography does to women is misleading on two counts. First of all, hurt is not a "reality" anyone has demonstrated--there is in this respect nothing to consider, and secondly, obscenity law cannot be accused of being part of a greater conspiracy aimed at women in particular for the reason that obscenity law has never considered the real harm which expression does to anyone of either gender. Anthony Comstock, the most successful censor in American history, was particularly concerned with the harm he said literature inflicted upon children, yet he "never was called upon to prove that the thing he called 'corrupting' was actually capable of achieving the dire results he predicted" (Broun 268), and the Canadian Supreme Court did not call upon MacKinnon or anyone else for proof either. If obscenity does indeed hurt innocent people, it is ultimately the innocent and harmless persons whom the state has the power to punish on the grounds that their speech or behavior is obscene.

In the latter half of the twentieth century the issue of actual harm has arisen with renewed urgency, and there are I believe two main reasons for this. The first is that the social sciences have developed methods for testing the possible impact of expression on behavior. As we have seen countless studies on the effects of something like pornography have been conducted throughout the world. The second is that both defenders and opponents of censorship have sought to use these studies to their advantage, but only for the reason that for the first time in centuries the issue of actual harm has been seriously reconsidered as the only acceptable justification for censorship. So even if the law, as we have seen, skirts the issue of harm, we can still ask the question, Do censors have any reliable evidence for believing that obscene expression causes actual harm?

The censors have lately tried quite hard to find such evidence. And why? Because as European and American societies have developed an increasing tolerance toward divergent moral opinion, many people and organizations have called for the elimination of laws which criminalize expression and conduct solely on the grounds that some find it offensive. In response, contemporary censors contend that their objections should not be mistaken for traditional opposition to divergent moral values. Mackinnon, for example, claims that for her "what is obscene is what harms women, not what offends our values" (qtd. in *New York Times*, Feb. 28, 1992). Seeking to distance themselves in the public's view from the kind of religious fundamentalism and moral puritanism which has fallen out of favor with many, contemporary censors have responded to the more liberal climate by attempting to offer a sound secular justification for censorship. If many now accept that society has no right to restrain individuals except for the purpose of preventing injury, then the censor, to be successful, would need to demonstrate injury. As Carole Vance noted of the *Meese Commission* the "chief supporters and beneficiaries of the commission were conservatives and fundamentalists whose main objection to pornography is its depiction of sex . . . outside of marriage. The Justice Department knew that this position would no longer sell. . . . The attack on sexually explicit material had to be modernized. . . . So the pre-eminent harm that pornography was said to cause was not sin and immorality but violence" (88).

To help them in their stated opposition to harmful expression, contemporary censors have had at their disposal the results of countless studies from numerous countries and they have tried to contend for decades now that there is reliable evidence that expression which they target for censorship causes real, measurable harm to individuals. The problem they confront is that even though numerous experimental psychologists and social scientists have searched high and low, and often mostly low, to find evidence of actual harm, no reliable evidence of harm has ever been found to exist! "We supply the ideology," Susan Brownmiller had said, "it's for others to come up with the statistics." But no one has been able to come up with statistics that would support the anti-porn ideology. So how have the censors responded to this paucity of evidence? After all is said and done, they have indeed adjusted their position like any good ideologist might. Ideology rarely considers evidence or is swayed much by it, but if confronted with a conflict between one's ideas and the evidence, an ideologist rarely admits that, in view of the evidence, his or her ideas must be considered incorrect. He or she either dismisses the evidence or people themselves (through inquisitions, pogroms, final solutions, show trials) rather than admit his or her ideas are ill-founded. So the answer, the "solution" the contemporary censor offers is to dismiss altogether the need for reliable evidence.

Consider this typical response by newspaper columnist, James Kilpatrick. In April, 1967, he testified before *The House of Representatives Select Subcommittee on Education.* "I am convinced," he said, "that this traffic in hardcore pornography is indeed an evil of considerable magnitude. . . . I cannot prove that it is harmful even to young people, but I doubt that the contrary can be proved either--that it is not harmful. There are times when reasonable men have to rely on their instincts and upon their common sense." As he would later write, "Common sense is a better guide than laboratory experiments; and common sense tells us pornography is bound to contribute to sex crime . . ." (*Lincoln* [Nebraska] *Evening Journal*, January 3, 1975). One can hardly imagine that Kilpatrick would dismiss laboratory experiments, that silly business about having to prove things, were their results consistent with rather than contrary to his intuitive beliefs. And the reason he pleaded for guidance from common sense to replace that of laboratory experiments is also obvious: Five years earlier *The Presidential Commission*, which found no evidence that sexual material caused harms of any kind, nevertheless reported that the "belief that reading or viewing explicit sexual materials causes sex crimes is widespread among the American public" (269). Charles Keating knew what the Commission report said regarding the disparity between evidence of harm and public perception, and, as we saw, he dismissed the absence of scientific evidence of harm as irrelevant. He, like Kilpatrik and so many others, insisted that in matters of censorship the law ought to be based not on evidence (certainly not on evidence that demonstrated no harm), but should defer, as it always had, to folk wisdom on the subject: In response to the *Commission Report* based upon numerous expert studies, Keating noted in remarks added to the published report itself that no matter what "all the experts" say and "studies" show "the fact that obscenity corrupts lies within the common sense . . . of every man."

Indeed as Bernard Arcand notes (citing the research of Ruth McGaffey on English and American obscenity trials), expert testimony has relatively little influence over common sense when juries deliberate issues of obscenity:

> Whereas in cases of homicide expert witnesses often exert a considerable influence over the jury, the opinions of witnesses from the same disciplines (psychiatry, sociology, and so on) suddenly become negligible when a court is trying to decide whether certain material is to be declared obscene. . . . Society affirms . . . that the modest individual, with neither title nor prestige nor any particular expertise in any recognized field, has as much or even more right to an opinion than the most experienced experts. This is, in fact, extremely rare, since in most other situations that same average individual cuts an ignorant figure that science must enlighten, if not crush under the weight of multiple-expert round tables. (12-13)

So the censor is not only happy to ignore all the experts, but would gladly defer questions of censorship to a common sense of things which readily dismisses the conclusions of experts. And by the late seventies, the situation had not changed one bit with respect to the evidence. By then many feminists had added yet another reason for censoring sexually explicit material which also depended upon popular superstition more than scientific reasoning of any kind. As Ann Garry noted in 1978, "Although I know of no social scientist whose data support the position that pornography leads to an increase in sex calloused behavior and attitudes, this view has popular support." And she noted that the "inclusive view" from Supreme Court decisions to popular writings on the subject was that pornography leads to various harms women suffer and "we do not need social scientists to confirm or deny it" This, she notes, had become a very influential viewpoint whose disturbing feature was "the temptation to disregard empirical data when the data fail to meet the author's expectations" (64-5).

In their response to scientific evidence, modern censors typify not only the reaction of those who have always been unalterably opposed to obscenity, but in the larger perspective, their responses typify the kind of negative reaction which has often greeted scientific evidence ever since the beginning of modern science itself. There is nothing new nor very original in their reaction. We might recall that the belief that the sun went round the earth was widespread among the public at the time when Galileo was forced to recant the view that, contrary to all common sense, the earth in fact spun on its axis and actually moved round the sun. And in 1911 a Princeton physics professor rejected Einstein's four dimensional space-time continuum because any model of the universe must be constructed he said of elements "which are immediately perceived by the senses and which are accepted by everybody" (Pearce Williams 120). The scientific theories of Copernicus, Galileo, and Einstein violated common sense, and Darwin's violated more than just that. There were plenty of "reasonable" men who dismissed Galileo, Einstein, or Darwin and will continue to resist countless other major scientific discoveries for the simple reason that modern science is quite often counter-intuitive, as Galileo, the father of modern science, understood. He expressed "unbounded admiration for the greatness of mind of these men who conceived [the heliocentric system] and held it to be true . . . , in violent opposition to the evidence of their own senses . . . ."

Science poses such a great threat to so many because its conclusions need to be arrived at without regard or respect for our common sense view of ourselves and the world, and as a result, it often contradicts not only what our instincts and good sense tell us, but what many, often sacred traditions, not to mention common prejudices would have us believe as well. In the *Novum Organum,* one of the fundamental works of the new philosophy, as science was first called, Francis Bacon warned that people usually come to their conclusions before consulting experience and then "having first determined the question according to [their] will," they bend experience in accordance with their preconceptions. And he added that the corruption of science "by superstition and an admixture of theology is far more widely spread, and does the greatest harm . . ." (sections 63 & 65). Thus after two hundred years of the kind of scientific reasoning Bacon called for, John Henry Cardinal Newman was led to conclude that the tendency of reason is such that "[n]o truth, however sacred, can stand against it . . ." (*Pro Vita Sua,* chapt. 5). The "problem" with science ultimately has to do with more than simple common sense. Science challenges the conceptual frameworks and foundation myths upon which many societies are built and, perhaps what is more significant, the power of those whose status and authority is sanctioned by those myths.

In their refusal to give appropriate consideration to the appropriate scientific evidence, in their hostile reaction to evidence which contradicts the common sense prejudices they would exploit, contemporary censors typify the kind of fear and prejudice and persecution which modern science has had to confront from its very beginnings. The findings of scientific studies respecting pornography are no different from those of Galileo or Einstein: they have also had to confront opposition from instinct and common sense, as well as superstition, theology, sacred belief, and sincere religious conviction. But before we elevate common sense to the ultimate test of true and false, right and wrong, we need to recall that common sense has told us for centuries that Jews were perfidious, Negroes and women inferior, and homosexuals and witches fit for the flames, and theology and sacred belief usually helped fan those flames. That people's gut instincts commonly tell them that pornography is also a great evil doesn't make it any more true because a lot of people believe it or want desperately to believe it, any more than the commonly held view that the sun went round the earth meant that the earth really stood still. Perhaps some Galileo of the social sciences will one day write expressing his admiration for the greatness of mind of those who in the face of the violent opposition of those motivated by common sense and sacred belief held it to be true that non-whites and women were not inferior, that homosexuals are not diseased and that pornography causes no harm.

Consider Catherine MacKinnon's response to the scientific data. At a National Women and Law Conference in 1985 she stated, "Researchers and clinicians documented what women know from our lives: that pornography increases . . . aggression . . . , principally by men against women." Over the years many within and outside the feminist movement have pointed out that the evidence she assumes to be there actually does not exist. So MacKinnon has changed her position. She has responded to information which has repeatedly shown that no evidence of harmful effects can be found by noting that "there is no evidence that pornography does no harm" (*Words* 37). Coming from someone who has fought for years to censor pornography for the harms she claims it causes, this is probably the single most significant recent statement we have indicating that there is no evidence for the supposed harms of pornography! Who would know better if such evidence existed? If it did, Mackinnon would be citing it for us, and not be reduced to saying that we have no evidence pornography does not cause harm.

But more fundamentally, her statement and those like Kilpatrick's doubting that one can prove that expression is not harmful, misunderstand the nature of research itself. One does not design an experiment to prove that something (like a correlation between pornography and violence) does not exist. The Michelson-Morley experiment was not set up to see if they could *not* find the ether. They did not report that having tried as best they could to not find the thing that they succeeded and didn't find it, so therefore the ether did not exist. The Michelson-Morley experiment proved that the ether did not exist precisely because it sought to find it and could not. You do not try to prove nothing (that there is no evidence for harm), but something (that there is evidence for harm), and when you fail to prove it, that is in fact what you have found: "not finding what you were looking for *is* a finding. It is all too easy to continue thinking, 'I didn't find it this time, I'll keep on looking" (Henry 101). It is also hardly reasonable or logical to say after a failure to find a causal relationship that there is no evidence that a causal relationship does not exist. Proof can come just as convincingly from failed as from proven hypotheses, and so when just about everyone who tries to find a causal relation between pornography and violence fails to find one, that *is* the evidence that pornography does not harm.

Ursula K. Le Guin, in a piece reprinted in, of all places, the *ACLU Newsletter*, similarly points out, "No psychological or sociological study has proved, or disproved, a connection between pornography and sex crimes. . . ." But she concludes that when "evidence conflicts judgment must call on informed ethical perception." Informed by what?: Common sense? Instinct? Anti-porn feminist ideology?

Given the way in which censors have repeatedly sought to distort the meaning of absence of evidence, we need to be especially clear about what lack of evidence does and does not prove. If I did not rape a woman in the woods there will be no evidence in the woods that I did not rape her, and if pornography does not cause harm there will of course be, as we have noted, no evidence that it does not. But additionally, if an accuser can find no evidence to support her accusation and persists in making charges without supporting evidence, it is no point in her favor that others can find no evidence to refute a claim which is itself without foundation. Not only is absence of evidence no evidence of absence, it certainly is no proof of presence. If I have failed to prove that the moon is made of green cheese or that pornography harms, that ought for the moment at least to be the end of the argument because there simply is no evidence to support my contention.

Even if dozens of people foolishly should attempt to disprove what has already been shown to be an unfounded contention and cannot do it, that does not indicate, as Le Guin contends, conflict of evidence. The situation is still the same: there is still no evidence one way or another, that pornography harms or that there's cheese in the moon. A million people failing to disprove an unfounded contention do not make it one bit more true than if everyone simply ignored it once those who proposed it failed to marshal any supporting evidence.

To point an accusing finger at opponents of censorship for having no proof that pornographic and obscene expression causes no harm is not only untrue, but misleading as well. It shifts responsibility and scrutiny from where they rightly belong. The burden of proof always rests with those who make a claim, not with those who doubt it: It is no proof of God's existence that atheists cannot prove that She does not exist and no evidence for the harm of pornography that those who oppose censoring it have no evidence that it does not cause harm. All the evidence opponents of censorship need is the fact that censors can marshal no reliable evidence in their favor--as they repeatedly admit. And indeed if there is one outstanding fact which has characterized modern censorship for the last two hundred and fifty hundred years it is that censors have never been willing or able to present any reliable evidence that illicit expression causes harm.

That contemporary opponents of obscenity, like Mackinnon and Le Guin, now take the position that scientific evidence will no longer count is about the best evidence we have that no such evidence can be found to support their accusations. That they persist in their censorship campaigns without regard for scientific support is good evidence that harm is the siren they sound to gain attention and support, but the real fact of the matter is that they are motivated by political ideology and moral superstition more than by any informed concern for human suffering:

> But does one need scientific methodology in order to conclude that the anti-female propaganda that permeates our nation's cultural output promotes a climate in which acts of sexual hostility directed against women are not only tolerated but ideologically encouraged?
>
> (Susan Brownmiller, *Against Our Will*)

I would think the answer ought to be, Yes. If individuals have scientific methodology at their disposal and do not use it or dismiss the information that science has gathered when it proves disagreeable, choosing to defer instead to what they call common sense or informed ethical perception, we have every right to question whether these individuals are in any way informed in their opinions or ethical in their actions. When ethical judgments are rendered without evidence to support them that does not constitute informed opinion. That is prejudice plain and simple, particularly when the evidence we do have suggests the judgement is ill-founded and perhaps even contrary to the facts of the matter. It does not matter whether the target group is women, the poor, racial minorities, homosexuals or consumers of pornography. It is still prejudice. And moral prejudice (often praised as common sense) remains the censor's chief motivator and his final court of appeal today as it has been since ancient times.

But what is even more disappointing is to find that the very feminists who are critical of those who ignore, misinterpret or dismiss the evidence usually do not allow the evidence to influence their own opinions either. Alice Henry (quoted above) knows what research has *not* found, but still supports tactics like picketing sex shops and smashing their windows (103). Julienne Dickey points out that the belief that pornography causes rape "is based on theory, not on sound evidence. In the absence of such evidence, *this may not be a bad thing,* but it must be recognised for what it is." And she then goes on to recommend one "way to effect the permanent elimination of pornography" (165-6, my italics). And she and Gail Chester point out that "we need to be quite clear that there is little *scientific* evidence [for the argument that pornography causes harm]. We have to use other, *feminist* arguments" (5). Why continue to support actions against sex shops when you well know that research has found no evidence that their merchandise causes harm? How is it a good thing to persist in promulgating a theory not based upon evidence? Why seek the permanent elimination of pornography when there is no sound evidence that it causes things like rape? If the problem is that the argument for harm has no scientific basis, why replace it with a feminist argument, unless an argument not based on evidence is preferable to one that seeks to be? If there is no scientific evidence for anything of any kind, there is absolutely no justification for any reasonable, honest, and responsible woman or man to insist that everyone else must accept it as true! Reason, good sense, and fairness requires that they, at least for the time being and until they or someone else uncovers new evidence, abandon their unsupported claims and desist from their unjustifiable actions--like breaking windows.

Neither Socrates nor Lord Cockburn had any psychological or sociological studies to show that it was wrong for the lower classes to read what the upper classes enjoyed and discussed. Their judgments were based upon prejudices which had no scientific support. The judgment of contemporary censors, like MacKinnon or LeGuin, are of course different. They differ for the reason that they result from prejudices retained in open disregard and explicit defiance of the psychological and sociological evidence the women are well aware of. And what is most disturbing is that the courts, when they agree to censor expression, do what would be abominable in most all other cases: they readily rule in favor of prejudice, intuition, common sense, the "reasonably" uninformed person, or community standards as a fitting substitute for actual proof. Thus the U.S. Supreme Court (*Paris Theatre I v. Slaton,* 1973) ruled that "[a]lthough there is no conclusive proof of a connection between antisocial behavior and obscene material, the legislature of Georgia could quite reasonably determine that such a connection does or might exist." The Canadien Supreme Court would later use the identical reasoning. For *Butler,* as we have seen, similarly ruled that it would sufficient "for Parliament to have a reasonable basis for concluding that harm will result and this requirement does not demand actual proof of harm." How the basis that something is correct can be called reasonable without even the requirement, let alone the proof that it is actually true is beyond me and, I would hope, every other reasonable and fair minded person.

The extent to which the practice of law generally proceeds on a rational basis is surely open to doubt, yet no area of law seems so deferential to human irrationality as does censorship law. We ordinarily require that the rulings and opinions of judges and juries be based upon the facts in the case. What the facts in a censorship case are is, as we have seen, at best uncertain and perhaps finally irrelevant to the extent that censorship law does not ordinarily insist that convictions be based upon the facts, but upon the presumptions or prejudices people hold respecting those facts. Prosecutors in such cases are not burdened with the need to prove that expression is *in fact* obscene or pornographic or that it does *indeed* cause harm. When it comes to questions of obscenity the correspondence is not between the opinion of a judge or jury and the factual evidence presented. When Potter Stewart said that he could not intelligibly define pornography, he recognized (or at the very least we may recognize from his remarks) that pornography was not something that had an objective existence independent of any and all observers, so he refrained from defining it in those terms. He no doubt understood that pornography exists only to the extent that someone sees and thinks he knows it to be such. Just as Lord Devlin knew morality is what twelve English men and women say it is, so pornography is solely what someone declares to be pornographic after he has seen it. The same is true for obscenity or blasphemy or hostile sexual environment. The law has always said that since these issues finally do not allow for the introduction of factual evidence one may defer to opinion without regard to whether or not that opinion corresponds to any facts. In the absence of factual evidence, the opinion may be legitimate if it corresponds not to facts but to community standards, or traditions, or conventions, or prejudices.

That obscenity is dangerous is not the only presumption shared by many. That black Americans are welfare cheats, or that women and Latinos are intellectually inferior or that Muslims in the United States present a threat to national security is also widely held by many Americans, but would we tolerate a ruling which stated that a legislature would have free reign to pass laws merely on the supposed reasonable or common sense assumption that these things were true and that it could do so without any actual proof that they were indeed true? I suspect even many Americans who do hold such opinions still know better than to wish them writ into law. At the end of the twentieth century we still do tolerate many such rulings regarding homosexuals, but even those who favor such rulings also know enough not to want them to form the basis of government policy regarding any and all classes of citizens. They clearly want to carve out a field of law for special groups--so much for equal justice under law. The same holds true for censorship law. Even if we often fail to eliminate irrationality and prejudice from legal matters, we still hold to the principle that a reasonable commitment to factual evidence, without regard to prejudice, is one of the best safeguards we posses for maintaining the rule of law. Yet we make regular exceptions when it comes to censorship law, not simply in practice but in the formation of the law itself. We admit that convention and prejudice will be the final arbiter of whether or not any form of expression may be deemed illicit.

Michael Gazzaniga, a leading neurobiologist, after reviewing numerous studies on the nature of and the mental processes involved in belief, writes that the "human capacity to hang on to our beliefs in the presence of confounding data is astounding. . . . We human beings . . . readily generate causal explanations of events and actively seek out, recall, and interpret evidence in a manner that sustains our personal beliefs. This tendency . . . has been shown [in laboratory experiments] to be true even under circumstances in which such causal explanations have no empirical foundation" (136). Those censors who claim that obscenity, or blasphemy, or pornography can produce actual harms represent some of the best examples of the preservation of belief without empirical foundation and in the presence of confounding data. I of course recognize that I or just about any other believer could be open to the same charge, but I think that, whatever other psychological or sociological factors might be involved, censors tend to represent these tendencies more than others if for no other reason than that censorship law has been fashioned to encourage these tendencies. It does so because (as we shall see in the next section) censorship is essentially about the preservation of belief. Censorship assumes the right of societies to assert, maintain, and enforce certain beliefs regardless of the fact that there may be no empirical evidence for them (that God is just and heaven awaits the believer) or that they are confounded by the data (that all men are created equal or that communism yields superior economic results). One can always tell which beliefs a society considers most important by seeing which ideas they censor most--whether it be ideas respecting politics, religion or sex; and it is telling that in modern bourgeois societies it is not ideas regarding politics or religion that are most likely to be suppressed. The fabric of bourgeois society is held together by particular beliefs we have regarding sexuality, and in view of the perceived importance of those beliefs the law allows that they need to be preserved and those opinions contrary to them must be suppressed even if there exists no empirical foundation for the beliefs one seeks to maintain through censorship.

But when it comes to preserving belief without support and dismissing confounding evidence, neither Catherine MacKinnon nor the Canadian Supreme Court can match *The Final Report of the Attorney General's Commission on Pornography (The Meese Commission)*. It remains the best current illustration of how allusions to scientific research are used to lend legitimacy to traditional censorship aims and practices and how the evidence is mishandled and finally ignored in favor of personal prejudice.

The objectives of the commission revealed that from the start the committee, stacked as it was with anti-porn crusaders, was going to use scientific research to bolster its claims, but had in fact made up its collective mind before ever considering the evidence. The very charge to the committee called for it at one and the same time to review "the available empirical and scientific evidence on the relationship of exposure to pornographic materials and antisocial behavior" and to recommend ways of regulating what it was already calling "the problem of pornography." The conclusion that pornography needed to be controlled was drawn prior to the review of any evidence:

> The objectives of the Commission are to determine the nature, extent, and impact on society of pornography in the United States, and to make specific recommendations to the Attorney General concerning more effective ways in which the spread of pornography could be contained . . . .

Worse yet, the commission discovered what a number of other anti-porn crusaders had already confronted, the fact that if they pinned their hopes for renewed censorship upon scientific evidence supporting their contention of harm, decades of research had already failed to support any such claim. So the commission did what other censors had already done. It turned against not only the scientific evidence that was readily available, but the very idea of the need for scientific evidence itself. The fault of the 1970 *Commission on Pornography* whose conclusions the *Meese Commission* was set up to counteract was, according to committee member, Park Elliot Dietz, that a majority of its members

> took the absence of experimental evidence of causation of antisocial behavior or sexual deviance as a basis for urging the deregulation of obscenity. The present Commission did not limit its inquiry to the products of social science research. . . . Every time an emperor or a king or a queen or a president or a parliament or a congress or a legislature or a court has made a judgment affecting social policy, this judgment has been made in the absence of absolute guidance from the social science.

Father Bruce Ritter went even further to criticize his own committee for limiting itself too much to the products of social science research. Its "fatal flaw," he wrote, was to base its conclusion "on evidence of harms drawn from the empirical and social sciences to the virtual exclusion of other kinds of 'evidence'." And he too appealed to the supposedly rational man or woman whom he was sure would accept the Commission's negative conclusions regarding violent and degrading pornography "quite apart form any 'evidence'," apart from any need "to 'prove' it."

Ritter's interpretation does not reflect what many felt to be one of the real flaws of the committee's work, that it gave inordinate importance to anecdotal evidence, to the testimony of distraught witnesses who claimed the harms they suffered were caused by pornography, and the commission publicized these claims with unquestioning credulity. The reliability of this "evidence" was never seriously challenged or publicly scrutinized. Rather, as we note, more than one committee member felt compelled to diminish the significance in such studies of the importance given to empirical and social science evidence, but not the reliability of emotionally charged testimony from tearful women. In the case of *The Meese Commission* it would seem that the scientific evidence it was charged to consult limited the kinds of strong anti-pornography measures committee members would have liked to recommend. Be that as it may, the pattern, familiar to modern arguments for censorship, of dismissing the significance of disagreeable scientific evidence runs throughout the work of the commission.

To use experimental evidence as "a basis" for one's recommendations is of course not to "limit" one's inquiry to science research or seek "absolute guidance" from it. Certainly, while it is true that the social policies of let's say the Inquisition or the Nazi party or the Ku Klux Klan, that tortured witches, burned homosexuals, gassed Jews, or hanged Negroes were carried out in the absence of guidance from the social sciences, the Meese Commission did seek guidance from the social sciences--it was in fact charged to do so--and chose finally not to be guided by them because they failed to support their own moral prejudices. When the evidence was in and found wanting with respect to the issue of harm, the Commission either ignored the evidence: "we do not deceive ourselves into thinking that the sample before us is an accurate statistical reflection of the state of the world," but we can still identify pornography as problematic "as long as one does not draw statistical or percentage conclusions from the evidence." Or else, in the words of the committee chairman, Henry E. Hudson, having found "a scarcity of definitive research on negative effects" of pornography, the report simply reverted to the three hundred year old legal presumption respecting obscenity, which is that something which cannot be proven to be harmful or for which there may even be evidence that it causes no harm whatsoever can nevertheless still be criminalized solely on the grounds that it offends someone's sense of good taste and decency:

> Issues of human dignity and human decency [Hudson wrote], *no less real for their lack of scientific measurability,* are . . . central to thinking about the question of harm. And when we think about harm in this way, there are acts that must be condemned not because the evils of the world will thereby be eliminated, but because conscience demands it.
>
>   Although the distinction between the two [harm and offence] is hardly clear, *most people can nevertheless imagine things that offend them, or offend others, that still would be hard to describe as harms. . . .* [W]e take the offensive to be well within the scope of our concerns. (my italics)

Over three hundred years ago the Attorney General of England successfully presented pretty much the same argument for making offensiveness a crime under common law with the result that throughout modern society the law allows that what is offensive to some members of society can justifiably be outlawed as wrong for everybody, regardless of the fact that others may not find it offensive or are not noticeably or measurably harmed by it. The law also allows for this despite the fact that while censors often insist on little or no difference between harm and offence, just about everybody, including people like Henry Hudson, clearly recognize the difference. One doesn't have to make an obscene gesture to Mr. Hudson's face one day and strike him on the nose with a ballpeen hammer the next to make him realize the difference. One only has to recite his own words, for if the distinction between harm and offence is hardly clear, how is it that most people clearly do not confuse the two and find it hard to describe things that offend them and others as harms? The 1970 Commission did not seek absolute guidance form the social sciences, but the chairman of the Meese Commission suggested that it sought absolute guidance from another source: It would condemn what conscience demanded ought to be condemned.

In the face of overwhelming evidence against their position, censors, like Hudson, often retreat to a fall-back position. They contend that even though there is no *measurable* evidence that obscene, blasphemous, or pornographic expression causes harm, it does cause *immeasurable* harm to human dignity and decency. But that view won't stand much scrutiny either. Censorship law may succeed by blurring the distinction between offence and harm and censors may thrive on the confusion, but the difference is quite clear to anyone who has been both offended and harmed.

First of all, to say that pornography produces changes and that these changes are no less real for lack of scientific measurability is rather misleading. It plays upon a notion popular with many that some things lie beyond the grasp of science, as if that in and of itself is some kind of negative reason for assuming something positively exists. Of course we are right to assume that many things do lie beyond science, but then we are for that reason less likely to know what they really are and have no right to assume that scientific ignorance can stand in for some kind of proof of one's one beliefs. God or unicorns cannot be said to exist for the reason that nobody can prove that She or they do not exist. But more importantly, the argument for immeasurable things misdirects us from the fact that the changes illicit expression supposedly produces are not only immeasurable; they are also not in any way observable. They make themselves no more available to the perceptions of the layman than they do to the instruments of the scientists. What we are actually being asked to accept for real is something which no one has ever measured *or* observed.

I do not mean to say that there is no such thing as real harms to human dignity, just that when people claim that they actually do occur we would expect to be able to observe them in some way or other. That we can and do in fact observe effects upon human dignity when they really do occur shows how completely wrong censors are when they claim such effects can result from what one reads and hears. The real harms to human dignity which slavery, prison camps, rape, torture, warfare, destitution, disease, drug addiction, sexual abuse and family violence produce are noticeable, long term, and often irremediable; and they can be observed and have been measured in terms of diffidence and lowered self-esteem, affectlessness, self-hatred, proclivity to violence against self and others, recurrent nightmares and other sleep disorders, increased suicide rates, permanent damage to mental and bodily functions, and a whole variety of psycho- and socio-pathological disorders. Nothing like that has ever been documented to occur as a result of exposure to blasphemous, obscene, or pornographic expression, and unless coached or otherwise influenced by opponents of such material, those exposed to it do not report, nor in any observable or measurable way do they suffer any degradation to mind and body. What changes, if any, such exposure produces, certainly produces nothing like what   is noticeable in victims of real indignities.   To identify obscene expression as producing immeasurable harm to human dignity is not simply a mistake and a patent absurdity, it is an insult both to individuals who have suffered real indignities as well as those who personally prefer what others simply do not like.

The often cited fact that pornography is a multi-billion dollar a year business might very well be proof that those millions of consumers who can afford to indulge this widespread taste for titllitaion are readily capable of maintaing their jobs, their families, and their dignity. When Hannah Tillich, the widow of Paul Tillich, revealed her husband's abiding interest in pornography and New York sex shows, anitiporn feminists like Robin Morgan were up in arms. Yet Paul Tillich remained till the time of his death one of the leading and most respected theologians of the twentieth century. Philip Larkin loved the "girlie mags" as he called them, and it in no way appears to have hurt him or his ability to carry out his role as poet laureate of England. There are those (like David Mura quoted below) who decry pornography as an addiction. Technically, at the very least, it is no such thing. Pornographic material is not a substance one consumes. It produces no long-term physiological changes and therefore no physiological dependency nor tolerance such that one experiences withdrawal symptoms if the material is removed, even if one goes "cold turkey" and has it removed suddenly and not in gradual stages. Individuals do not, as we often hear nowadays, build up a tolerance to pornography as addicts do to drugs so that they come to crave stronger doses of presumably more violent kinds in order to be satisfied. What mostly men crave in sexual experience is variety. Like it or not, what men desire is not more and greater thrills from the same woman, but to do the same thing with someone else. If the former were the case then magazines like *Playboy* would not need to come out with a new playmate every month, but could just feature Miss January in increasingly extreme situations throughout the year, with the December issue being regularly its biggest seller. This pattern of male desire is a running gag in the popular television sitcom *Married with Children*, where Al Bundy is constantly drooling over numerous women while being completely indifferent to the sexual advances of his wife. In fact the pattern of diminishing desire with extended familiarity is so much a part of male sexuality that scientists have a name for it: they call it "the Coolidge effect" (see Glen Wilson's book of that title), and it is found in laboratory rats as well as husbands like Bundy who wander to other women. If this means that when it comes to sex, men are no better than rats, one is after all entitled to her opinion, but such behavior says a lot about the nature of male sexuality and nothing about the effects of pornography, for when it comes to sexuality men can get just as bored with the women they know as the magazines they own and this should not be taken as proof that the women or the magazines are of poor quality, nor that a man might not value a woman for characteristics beyond mere sexual appeal.

The "consumption" of pornography may of course in some cases involve obsessive-compulsive disorders which *The Diagnostic and Statistical Manual of Mental Disorders-III* describes as repetitive and stereotyped behavior. These may take many forms, such as compulsive gambling, shopping or hand washing, but we are now coming to find that such behavior patterns, which have been successfully controlled through drug therapy, are more likely innately generated than the result of experience. Besides, *DSM-III* goes on to say that "obsessions or compulsions are a significant source of distress to the individual or interfere with social or role functioning," but all the evidence suggests that people like Tillich and Larkin typify those who consume pornography and they do not find it a source of stress or interference. The typical consumer is not typically more distressed than anyone else (if guilt is not inculcated into him by others), is no more a social misfit or a rapist (rapists, studies show, tend to have *less* early exposure to sexual material), and next to the relatively rare rapists who may also coincidentally possess pornographic material (how many single men these days don't, and what rapist before the 1800's did?), the typical consumer offers statistical proof by the overwhelming millions that pornography involves harmless enjoyment that produces changes no more lasting than an endorphin rush and a good night's sleep.

Of course the prevailing ideology says otherwise. In the 1989 preface to her book *Pornography*, Andrea Dworkin compares the experience of women working in pornography with what Frederick Douglas and Sojourner

Truth knew under slavery, what Primo Levy and Elie Wiesel suffered in the Nazi concentration   camps, and what Nadezshda Mandelstam and Aleksander Solzhenitsyn bore witness to about the Soviet gulags. I have read Nadezshda Mandelstam's *Hope Against Hope*, Elie Wiesel's *Night*, Primo Levy's *Survival in Auschwitz*, and Aleksander Solzhenitsyn's *One Day in the Life of Ivan Denisovich*. I have read additional books by them and other authors detailing some of the worst horrors of this or any century. And do you know what? I have not read or heard of anyone who survived the camps saying it was like working in pornography. Under American slavery, under fascist, Nazi and Stalinist rule, what people witnessed and suffered were separation from friends and family, forced labor under hardly bearable, life threatening conditions, imprisonment without trial, repeated and systematic torture, survival on insects and servings of boiled grass, starvation, "medical experiements" involving inserting cement into the uterus or removing the top of the victim's skull to perform "brain sugery" with the "patient" fully conscious. People were hanged, eloctrocuted, buried alive, burned alive, and gassed to death. In all, anywhere from thirty to forty million people died as a result. Only a disordered and irresponsible mind could compare such horrible suffering and death to what women experience in pornography--disordered if Dworkin and others are actually convinced by their rhetoric, irresponsible if they are deliberately making hyperbolic and vicious comparisons to stigmatize whoever and whatever they personally obejct to.

It certainly might be more accurate to say that women in the porn industry are being exploited, and one might conceivably compare what they experience to the exploitation of coal miners or sweat shop and migrant farm workers. Or what of the worldwide exploitation of female gymnasts? Young teenage and pre-teen girls well under the age of consent whose bodies are forced through punishing, dangerous routines, which often result in serious, crippling injury. These girls are not treated with disrespect, nor is their sport vilified. Indeed it requires quite an imaginative stretch even to compare women in the porn industry with other exploited laborers. An hour or so in bed simulating or performing sex can't compare in terms of pain and injury to a day's work in the mines, the gym. or the steel mills. The real hurt, one must suppose, comes from the rejection and disrespect these women suffer, even--perhaps especially-- from those who claim to defend their interests. Like everyone else, what these woman want is respect. They are after all doing honest work for an honest dollar, more honest than most of the salespeople we deal with, the politicians we support, or the religious leaders we honor. It is ironic that feminists among others have cautioned us against blaming the victim, and yet they continue to heap blame upon women within the sex industry whom they would have the rest of us recognize as victims. It is ironic and shameful that the women who claim to be concerned with what these women supposedly suffer probably regard their sisters in the industry with more disdain than the men they claim are exploiting them.

So if one truly believes that exploitation is the problem and is sincerely concerned about it, the solution would be not to waste everyone's time composing articles and statutes on censorship. Censoring pornography would eliminate a source of income for many women, and by driving pornography back underground it would expose them once more to the violence they did suffer from police, pimps and others when pornography was strictly illegal (see McElroy, esp. Chapt. 6 for a discussion of this problem). The solution is to see that other opportunities are open to women so that they might compete with men on an equal footing and eventually receive equal pay for equal work. And for those who still choose to work in pornography the answer would be what has always been the answer to the exploitation of labor: unionize the women and men within the industry! A labor union for anyone working within the sex industry to provide them with good working contracts, safe working conditions, appropriate grievance procedures, fair pay and solid health benefits would seem to be the most appropriate and humane response to many of the problems sex workers might or do experience. But those who claim concern for what women suffer rarely, if ever offer any solution but censorship. It would be comparable to someone "solving" the problem of low pay, insecurity, and poor working conditions among factory workers in the United States by closing down all the factories in the country.

As pornography has moved out from under the counter to become a major legal industry within the United States women in it perform under better working conditions, are not subject to violence, or if they are, it tends to come from where it used to regularly come, that is, from the police. Women are beginning to work under contracts, although it does not seem likely that any court would presently uphold them. By far, as one one porn star reported to Wendy McElroy, "A union would be the best sort of contract we could get" (157).

There are remedies for real hurt and harm which sex workers and organizations like COYOTE, which actually do speak for actual women, have been asking for, but some feminists who claim to be genuinely concerned with what women suffer in the pornography industry reject remedies of any kind. Lenore Tieffer has noted that these "women have appealed to feminists for support, not rejection. . . . Sex industry workers, like all women, are striving for economic survival and a decent life, and if feminism means anything it means sisterhood and solidarity with these women" (qtd. in McElroy 144). But of course that is not what feminism has come to mean for many. In the United States and elsewhere feminism has been a leading force for censorship of sexual material. The reason is not simply that for many, feminism has shifted from an earlier movement for sexual liberation to a puritanical and gender hostile agenda. Many anti-censorship and sexual freedom feminists are just beginning to point this out, and I would recommend to those who think Dworkin or MacKinnon do indeed speak for all women and do define what feminism is all about that they read the writings of Carole Vance, Nadine Strossen, or Susie Bright, among many others, to see that feminism, like any social-political movement, is not monolithic or without its internal differences. Indeed, attacks upon sexually explicit expression and calls for its censorship have been a leading cause for division and strife among feminists, and it has in the long run proved a considerable set-back for the movement for woman's rights.

But more fundamentally, I believe, a general problem with feminism in terms of its acceptance of censorship is that it was rather early on co-opted by women within academia and as a result quickly degenerated from a force for political, social, and economic change which would benefit all women to an ideology enamored, like most all ideologies are, with catch phrases and powerful rhetoric. As a result, large parts of the movement lost sight of any real concern for the actual persons these ideologues claimed to care about and any regard for factual information (a lot of feminist "scholarship" is some of the most absurd some of us have ever seen). By comparison the civil rights movement, although it has spawned some goof ball notions, mostly again from academics, has remained true to its initial aims of economic and social justice for black and other minorities within the United States. (Indeed it could be argued that women in general have benefitted as much from the civil rights movement as from the feminist movement. For example, the chief beneficiaries of affirmative action programs have arguably been white females.) But by degenerating from a political movement to an ideolgical forum, feminism became more interested in furthering certain ideas rather than advancing the cause of women in general. And perhaps inevitably when its concern tended to focus upon the realization of a correct ideology it turned, as almost all ideologies do, to censoring those types of expression whose attitudes, values, and opinions it regarded as heretical and unorthodox. Needless to say, not all feminists ran that route, but many did, and I think it explains why so many became advocates in this country and elsewhere for censorship. The reason wasn't simply their disgust with male sexuality nor their supposed concern with violence against women. The fundamental reason was that they had become ideologues seeking to outlaw the expression of ideas which did not conform to their ideologies.

There should be nothing surprising about ideological feminism masking itself as a movement concerned for the well-being of individual women, even as it seeks above all to get all women ultimately to conform in their opinions and choices to its beliefs. Most all censorship has as its stated aim the well-being of others, the concern that their souls might otherwise burn in hell for all eternity or that everyone's progress towards the communist utopia will be set back. The nature of ideology is such that it supposes man-made suffering will end and benefits accrue when people come to adhere to a predetermined set of beliefs--if they give lip service to the apostolic creed or the truths of Marxist-Leninism--and as a result they are responsible for much, if not most of the suffering men have inflicted upon other men and women throughout history.

In *Roth v. the United States, 1956,* Judge Jerome Frank noted, that to "date there exist . . . no thorough-going studies by competent persons which justify the conclusion that normal adults' reading or seeing of the 'obscene' probably induces anti-social conduct." We have seen that judgment has been reconfirmed many times since, and there still exists no thorough-going studies by competent persons to refute it. Yet, Terrence J. Murphy responded to the judge's observation by remarking, "The kernel of the argument [against censoring material that might prove harmful] is that ideas have no consequences. At least, ideas received from reading and visual matter have no consequences" (qtd. in Widmer 76 & 79).

For sure, no one can reasonably say that exposure to obscene or pornographic literature has no consequences, but that is not what Judge Frank said. What he and others have repeatedly pointed out is that there is no evidence that *one* of the consequences of obscene material is that it induces anti-social conduct. To deny one consequence because there has never been reliable evidence for it is not to deny any and all consequences. But the significant fact of the matter is that those who would censor claim that ideas received from visual and reading matter have *more* consequences. The response to such extraordinary claims is and ought to be not that ideas received from reading and visual matter have no consequences, but that there is no evidence for the claim that ideas received from illicit matter can produce consequences radically different from those that are ordinarily produced by any other genre of literature or art.

The argument is frequently given that if people believe art and literature can have beneficial effects upon people's lives, why can they not admit that it can also have harmful effects? Responding to the findings of *The Presidential Commission on Pornography,* which found no evidence for any connection between pornography and harmful effects and called for the elimination of laws regulating it, President Nixon said, If it were true that "the proliferation of filthy books and plays has no lasting harmful effect on a man's character, it must also be true that great books, great paintings and great plays have no ennobling effect on a man's conduct" (*New York Times,* Oct. 25, 1970).

First off, I suspect that both proponents and opponents of censorship make too much of the effects art and literature have, and I do not think the effect art and literature has upon the development of the individual can compare with good parenting or bad nutrition. For his or her purpose the censor tends to view books almost exclusively in moral terms. The benefits of good books would seem fairly obvious. They can entertain, make a person more knowledgeable, more interesting, better qualified for numerous job opportunities. By the way, the same can be said for filthy books, but what effect books of any kind have on the enhancement or degeneration of a man's or woman's moral character remains at best uncertain, if not doubtful. It is questionable just how much impact they have in building our moral character. In response to the censoriousness of Victorian society Oscar Wilde wrote (in his Preface to *Dorian Gray*) that a work of literature is neither moral nor immoral. I suspect he is probably correct. But in any event even if we accept the censor's position that books need to be understood primarily in moral terms there is still no reason to accept the unbalanced view they present. For what the censors claim is not that literature can produce effects. Censors going all the way back to Plato have not argued simply that art and literature can produce effects. What censors claim is that they can identify certain types of art or literature--poetry for Plato, rock 'n' roll for some parents, pornography for certain feminists-- which are so fundamentally different from other genres in the *extraordinary* effects they are capable of producing, effects which no other type of literature seems capable of producing, that extraordinary measures need to be taken against them and special legal categories which identify these genres as categorically different from all others--identify them as blasphemous, obscene, or pornographic material--need to be created to combat them and their effects.

Plato presented perhaps the first extended argument for censorship, and it is one that has been repeated down to our own day. In *The Republic* he attacked the popular art of his day for the same reasons popular culture has been attacked in our own. That popular art form was then poetry, and he banned poets from his republic because the "poet who aims at being popular ... implants an evil constitution" by appealing to the irrational: "poetry feeds and waters the passions instead of drying them up; she lets them rule, although they ought to be controlled, if mankind are ever to increase in happiness and virtue" (Book X, trans. B. Jowett). The point to note here is not simply that Plato talking about Homer sounds a lot like some judges or feminists talking about pornography or that now that Homeric poetry is an academic subject, almost everyone who does talk about Homeric poetry speaks of its benefits rather than harms. The point to note as well is that in *The Republic* Plato did not prohibit the reading of any and all literature, nor despite his denigration of the visual arts which he argued were equally poor in representing truth, did he call for preventing artists from practicing in his model state. He called specifically for a ban on poetry because he believed this one particular genre possessed extraordinary power which other types of literature and art did not have. They did not appeal to the irrational in men. They did not posses the power to alter men's conduct and adversely affect the virtue and happiness of mankind in the ways he believed poetry did.

If we accept that art and literature can produce both good and bad effects, there is still no reason to take for true the censors' contention that the genres they target produce effects radically different from any other genre, particularly since there is no proof that the incredible long term effects they claim for these genres actually do occur. All art, as Wendy Steiner has noted, "reproduce real effects such as laughing, crying, screaming, and accelerated heart rate. What makes something like pornography different and a target of censors is the particular effect it produces--sexual excitement--not that it can produce real physiological effects where no other genre can or that the effects it produces last any longer" (68).

While Steiner observations are true enough and important to note, we might add that an important difference for the censor is not only that pornography for instance produces sexual excitement, but that this excitement is presumed to last a long time after the experience of pornography itself. The physiological change is presumed not only to last longer than other effects which literature produces, but longer than the same effect (sexual excitement) if and when that effect is produced by an actual person. An exciting night with an exciting sexual partner is not presumed to have the long term disturbing effect that a ninety minute video produces. Thus we would immediately recognize all the following statements as absurd--all that is but the last:

A film of such frightening power I couldn't stop screaming for months!
The play left me laughing for years!
The novel was so thrilling that a week after finishing it my heart still hadn't
  settled down and I had to check into a hospital.
After I read my first pornographic novel, I didn't need to read any other. I
  was in a state of constant arousal, I could not sleep, eat or work, or tend
  to my family. I had to find some relief . . .

All variety of art and literature without exception have the power to produce physiological and emotional effects. But contrary to what censors claim for certain designated types, these effects are invariably short-lived, and no work of art or literature of any kind has ever been known to have the power to maintain the effects it produces for any extended period of time. The reason for this is quite simple and has to do ultimately with the nature of emotion more than literature. Emotions like anger, fear, or lust allow us to respond quickly and decisively to danger or opportunity (the term, *emotion,* like *motion,* derives from the same Latin root meaning to move). The persistence of emotions at their relatively intense level in the absence of appropriate, external stimuli is a sure sign of emotional disorder. Emotions may taper off into extended moods, as when sudden grief becomes persistent melancholy or intense passion turns into matrimonial comfort (or persistent melancholy), but if we were not constituted so that our emotions did not arise rapidly and disappear almost as quickly we would not be capable of responding to life's constantly and often quickly changing circumstances. The response of emotionally stable individuals to art is therefore no different from their response to any other stimulus: It may be mild or intense, but invariably short-lived. The same is true of emotionally or mentally unstable persons: Their response to art or literature may be exaggerated both in intensity and duration, but that is characteristic of the way they tend to respond to all other stimuli and says nothing about the power of art or literature to move people in ways that work differently from any other emotional stimulus.

Furthermore one expects and understands that people who are moved by sentimentality will tend to seek out and be moved by sentimental works, and that people who enjoy thrillers will also tend to seek out and be excited by them. We do not expect that cynics who laugh at sentimentality will likely be moved by it or that those disgusted by depictions of murder and mayhem will suddenly be turned on by thrillers. But we have been led to believe that people not susceptible to pornography or to particular sexual preferences will suddenly be moved and even modified by it, that by exposing them to a few pictures, heterosexuals will suddenly start frequenting gay bars, that people with sensitive stomachs will become coprophiles, and those with a preference for large, busty women will turn to pedophilia. Notice, we never hear that by showing men and women making love without paraphernalia pornography has the power to convert homosexuals or devotees of bondage and discipline into heterosexual lovers of the missionary position.

But pornography hasn't the power to do any of these things, since in fact pornography operates on and effects people no differently from what we would expect of any other work of art or literature. Based upon extensive research rather than folk wisdom, *The Presidential Commission on Obscenity and Pornography* concluded that exposure to erotica, if it resulted in anything, resulted in "a temporary activation of individuals' preexisting patterns of sexual behavior." It makes sense. A temporary activation of preexisting patterns of response and behavior, that is all *any* emotional stimulus usually causes and that is all we ordinarily expect any work of art or literature can cause, and obscene art or literature shows itself to be no different.

Another major reason for pornography's inability to change us is that sexual responses and behavior tend to be set quite early in one's development and to be pretty stable over time. Women especially may come to certain sexual awakenings after a considerable time (see Kate Chopin's masterpiece, *The Awakening,* for one excellent fictional account of a woman coming to recognize herself as a sexual being.), but just about every reader will recognize that his or her peculiar sexual preferences, fantasies, idiosyncracies, orientations, and turn-ons have been pretty much the same throughout his or her life. Most of us can recall that they go all the way back to childhood, before the onset of puberty or our exposure to prurient material. How they came about still remains a mystery. That they have not and most likely will not ever change is a practical certainty no matter what type of art or literature we are exposed to. Art or literature is neither degrading nor therapeutic with respect to anyone's sexuality. It does not shape our sexual preferences, alter them or make them disappear once they have been formed.

If art and literature have such power over people, then all art and literature should be outlawed for its potential danger. But censors never seek such blanket prohibitions. What they target is not literature capable of producing extraordinary effects. What they target is art and literature that contains ideas or responses they find disagreeable and then, because they find them disagreeable or offensive and wish to save from censorship the art and literature they do appreciate, they attribute to these works and these works alone a power beyond anything they or anyone else recognizes art or literature ordinarily to posses. The censor might say, as Nixon for one did, that if good books have ennobling effects, it must be true that filthy books have harmful effects. But do they honestly believe in a power of good books equal to the power they ascribe to bad ones? If they did then the appropriate response to the influence of bad books might very well be to encourage, especially youngsters to read more good books. This recommendation is obviously not the one we hear from the censor, probably for the reason that one does not tend to find among censors people who are primarily interested in books in the first place or who get must pleasure out of reading. They are people I suspect who from their own experience do not believe that good books can do very much good. Those in government who support censorship are also those who would curb or eliminate altogether funding for the arts or public broadcasting. So one is not likely to meet with much success by turning Nixon's argument around and asking of the censor, If filthy books can produce so much damage, why cannot good books correct the problems bad books create? Rather than censor what some feel might be harmful, why not allow people to read as many "harmful" books as one wants so long as it is balanced by an equal number of "beneficial" books? Even if exposure to pornography can seriously alter the human psyche, why do we need to censor it? Why can't all those books written about the evils of pornography work their white magic and cure those poisoned by pornography?

In *Seduction of the Innocent*, Dr. Wertham dismissed such a program with respect to comic books. He said that the "idea that by giving children something good to read, crime comics can be combated . . . has proved naive wherever it was tried. It does not take into account the mass character of the seduction, which is precisely why crime comic books are an entirely new phenomenon not equaled before at any time nor place" (312). No plan to combat bad books with good ones will work because good books to the censor's way of thinking are not thought to be *that* good. They certainly cannot equal the seductive power of bad books. Despite the extraordinary harms they claim for bad books censors usually do not make equally extraordinary claims for good books. They do not contend that reading them will produce beneficial results comparable to the harmful consequences bad books produce. We hear that bad books are or act like filth, disease, poison, and so on, but we never hear that good, clean reading can in and of itself cure disease, serve as an antidote to poison, or eliminate altogether unwanted human desires, and anyone who claimed the latter, unlike those who claim the former, would no doubt be laughed off almost any public stage and committed to the care of a psychiatrist. The censor believes that good books have beneficial effects and not-so-good books have little or no effect, but bad books produce effects that books don't otherwise have the power to produce: good books act like books, but bad books act, not like books, but like poison, filth, or disease.

The hyperbolic metaphors and similes used to describe bad literature and the extraordinary power attributed to it, simply do not extend to good literature. Thus despite the comparison Nixon and others make between the ennobling effects of great books and the harmful effects of filthy books, there is in their mind no comparison between the two: The censor's "logic" does not say that good and bad books confront each other at opposite ends of the reading spectrum, for to their way of thinking the benefits good reading can offer are not commensurate with, are categorically different form and thus can never equal the harms bad books can produce. In what might be called the taxonomy of censorship offensive expression is removed from the category of expression altogether and classified by its effects with poisons, contagious diseases, black magic and demon possession. Censors from Plato to Comstock to MacKinnon have argued that society needs to create a special category for certain types of expression which they say move us or act upon us in ways that are categorically different from the way other forms of expression work. It is naive "to believe that anything other words can do is as powerful as what pornography itself does," MacKinnon contends. "[N]othing else does what pornography does" (*Words* 108 & 15). Plato similarly believed that nothing else did what poetry did. Thus the need for special legal categories which treat select forms of expression as different from all other forms, as different indeed from expression itself.

Once more I would note that there are indeed special categories of individuals who might and do indeed respond to literature in criminal ways. They are not as noted above classes of people as most censorship rulings would have us believe. They are deranged individuals, and even for them there is no evidence that it is the particular kinds of expression people wish to censor which take possession of them in a way that is uniquely different from other forms. Censors argue that certain types of expression have the potential to drive anyone to evil deeds when the more apparent fact of the matter is that certain types of individuals can be driven to evil deeds by any type of expression. Heinrich Pomerenke, a rapist and mass murderer of women, committed his first murder after viewing *The Ten Commandments*, a film which convinced him that women were the source of the world's evils and needed to be punished for it. John George Haigh, who sucked his victims' blood through soda straws before dissolving their bodies in acid, was first led to have vampire dreams after watching the "voluptuous" Anglican High Church Communion Service. Had these men been exposed to pornography, God knows what atrocities they may have been driven to.

Interestingly enough the Marquis de Sade, to take an extreme case in point, was nothing like psychotics like Pomerenke or Haigh either in how he thought or acted. Marice Lever makes it rather clear that Sade's activities did not depart that much from the common practice of aristocratic libertines of the *ancien regime*. Police reports of the time indicate that many bordellos were well stocked with whips and similar paraphernalia for satisfying a common aristocratic taste. The first Frenchman to write against capital punishment and who decried the horrors of the September massacres during the revolution understood the differences between fantasy and action better than most. One does not have to defend Sade's crimes or appreciate his writings to recognize that the following statement was true for him as it will be for all sane individuals: "I have thought of everything that can be thought of . . . , but I have certainly not done everything I have thought of and surely never will" (Lever 204) What he did was bad enough, but he understood the differences between fantasy and action and knew the limits of what he could do. If he did what he did it was above all because he was a member of a society which for centuries had permitted noblemen to commit all kinds of crimes against men and women of the lower orders with impunity. The society after the Revolution was no less licentious. In fact it was probably more so insofar as pornographic works like Sade's *Justine*, published in 1797, were now available to a mass reading public where they had previously been the exclusive province of aristocratic taste. In 1797 one might have been able to read a whole stream of lewd works, but to commit the acts Sade did before 1789 was no longer tolerated and it simply wasn't done anymore.

In the end what matters most is not what one reads or believes. It matters what society will permit a man to do. A psychotic will be driven by anything he encounters in print, but that proves not the power of print but the impressionability of psychotics; and a psychotic will be deterred by nothing society condemns. A sane man, even one with a fevered libido like Sade's, will read and believe and desire and imagine what he will, but will know and be restrained in his actions by what society will and will not permit him to do.

If we were to take the censors at their word regarding the extraordinary, immeasurably harmful effects art and literature produce (since they can't show measurable effects), we would have to believe that some forms of art and literature posses powers not only beyond anything we ordinarily know art and literature to possess (except when it comes to psychotics), but which surpass anything we know just about anything to posses (except when it comes to psychotics). If the censor believes that certain forms of expression do indeed have the power to produce serious and wide ranging harm to individuals and society, the question then is how and through what agency is art and literature capable of producing these extraordinary effects? What exactly is the nature of this terrible power that art and literature possess?

Anthony Comstok, perhaps the most successful individual in the history of American censorship, offered a most revealing explanation as to how obscene literature works its extraordinary effects: "I unhesitatingly declare," he wrote in *Traps for the Young*, "there is at present no more active agent employed by Satan . . . to ruin the human family and subject nations to himself than EVIL READING." (240). Comstock makes it very clear why he believed bad books posses a power surpassing what other books and just about everything else posses. Reading bad books is the agency through which the devil himself works his evil! Of course I can't resist pointing out here that when it comes to working evil in this world all records we have dating back to biblical times reveal that infinitesimally less people have been persecuted, tortured, and killed by worshipers of Satan than worshipers of Yahweh, Christ, or Allah. If by their fruits ye shall know them, then the rotten fruit of devil worship can't compare with the suffering that has been brought down upon countless people in the name of God. When Comstock spoke of evil in this world, his concern I would suggest was not exaggerated. It was misdirected. He should have scrutinized believers like himself to discover what type of people are responsible for inflicting the most pain, suffering, and death upon the rest of humanity. Yet even though he said he literally believed in the devil, Comstock, writing in the modern and not the medieval age, had to admit that it "may not be. . .popular to speak of a devil, or of his having a kingdom and power . . . . I believe that there is a devil. Those who disagree with me may translate my language. . . . Let my language be considered symbolical, provided the evils I denounce are regarded as *diabolical"* (239).

Comstock made a most revealing offer. Fundamentalist believers could of course be expected to take everything he said literally, but he recognized that a literal belief in the devil was not the most credible notion for an audience of his day and so he offered that it might be more palatable to a modern, skeptical reader to translate what he took literally regarding the devil and his power into symbolic, figurative speech, but only on condition that they did not also take as figurative or symbolic the evil effects he claimed literature produced. These effects were to be recognized as real. In other words,

Comstock asked his readers to retain a literal belief in diabolical agency without literally believing in the devil.

There is a joke about a man so poor that he couldn't afford the cheese he needed for his mouse trap, so he cut out a picture of a piece of cheese and put it in the trap, only to wake up the next morning to discover that he had caught a picture of a mouse. Comstock's logic requires us to accept an equally absurd possibility, wherein that which is not the thing itself, but only a symbol of it, can still posses the same power, the same active agency of the thing it represents. The symbol of the thing can actually produce effects in the real world identical to those produced by that which it symbolizes. To accept Comstock's logic we would have to believe that if I struck someone on the head with a picture of a rock I could literally smash his skull, or that a picture of a trap could actually ensnare a young person. Of course, we might add, not just any picture could do the trick. It would have to be a picture designated by Comstock as possessing these powers. As not just any water is holy, but only that which the priest has blest, so any literature does not have the power to work evil, but only those works that are judged to be obscene or indecent, and they are usually not understood to posses this power until someone like Comstock comes along and declares them obscene. A declaration of obscenity or blasphemy invests expression with a power expression does not or did not ordinarily contain.

Those who contend that contact with indecent literature can produce serious harm to individuals and society are often talking, whether they know it or not, in terms of the logic of black magic and demon possession. Comstock was quite up-front about his belief in diabolical agency. Neither Dworkin nor Mackinnon so far as I know have ever referred to the devil or demonology in their censorship campaign--perhaps because they are too preoccupied documenting all the devilish things men ordinarily do. And yet when they seek to identify the damage pornography can do, there is nothing I know of besides the devil or plagues at their worst which can wreck such various and widespread havoc upon any society, nothing that is, except the violation of some taboo that would release some mysterious evil energy capable of destroying an entire society: Pornography according to Dworkin and MacKinon poses "a substantial threat to the health, safety, peace, welfare, and equality of citizens in the community. . . . The harm of pornography includes dehumanization, sexual exploitation, forced sex, forced prostitution, physical injury, and social and sexual terrorism and inferiority . . . ." It promotes "bigotry and contempt," fosters "acts of aggression," diminishes "opportunities for equality of rights in employment, education, property, public accommodations and public services," it creates "public and private harassment, persecution and denigration," it promotes "injury and degradation such as rape, battery, child sexual abuse, and prostitution and inhibit[s] just enforcement of laws against these acts," it damages "relations between the sexes" and undermines "women's equal rights to speech and action guaranteed" guaranteed under the Constitution and the laws of the United States ("Model Antipornography Law," see for example *Ms.*, April 1985, for just one reprinting of the model).

Women in America are indeed--no question about it--denied equal rights, and they are getting raped, and beaten, and abused, and murdered and while all this is going on Dworkin and Mackinnon are busy talking and writing about pictures, and they are trying to warn us that the pictures are causing all these things to happen. They would have us believe all this terror would diminish or perhaps even end if we could get rid of the pictures. However, there is some evidence that this overwhelming concern with pornographic representations has had quite the opposite effect. It has in fact diverted attention from the real problems of actual violence against women and how to prevent it. For example, New York City's Sergeant Harry O'Reilly, one of the nation's foremost experts on the investigation of sex crimes who helped set up that city's model rape unit, said that since feminists have moved on to other issues like pornography and aren't lobbying for rape prevention, "police departments have lightened up on the emphasis they had" on the crime of rape (reported in *The Chicago Reader*, November 15, 1985).

To counter that these are only pictures or only words doesn't get us very far with many modern censors, for as the title of Mackinon's book, *Only Words*, informs us, we are not dealing here only with words. Mackinon's aim for years has been to circumvent the special protections which words have under the First Amendment, but in the power, the agency she repeatedly ascribes to what others mistake to be only words and symbols, we can see that she would have us believe that words and symbols magically posses the power of the thing they symbolize and with that the demonic capacity to produce an incredible variety of harms throughout the entire society.

Comstock's literal belief in the devil may have been, as he himself admitted, incredible by modern standards, but whether we realize it or not, most all modern censorship campaigns have in fact adopted Comstock's proposal. For whether modern censors literally believe in the devil or find such belief to be outdated and incredible, everyone seems to have little difficulty when it comes to assigning diabolical agency to symbolic expression, which is exactly what Comstock proposed we do. But such thinking is no less "outdated" than a literal belief in the devil. For what

Comstock and other seemingly modern censors would have everyone accept is a return to mythic and superstitious methods of thinking.

As Cassirer has noted, "the mythic state of consciousness" understands "all verbal utterances" to posses "magical and daemonic power." Its belief in the "essential identity between the word and what it denotes" means that "the word . . . is not a mere conventional symbol, but is merged with its object in an indissoluble unity." The word is conceived as "a substantive being and power" (55, 49, 58, 62).

In *The Fear of the Word,* Eli M. Oboler has made a good case for understanding modern censorship as a remnant in contemporary societies of primitive religious taboos and the mythic modes of thought Cassirer analyzes. "Where violations of taboos occur, destructive powers are unleashed. Committing a tabooed deed brings defilement . . . ." Furthermore, he notes (quoting Westermarck), "'when an object is *taboo* it is supposed to be charged with mysterious energy that will injure or destroy the person who comes in contact with the forbidden thing . . . '" (9). But not the person only. The "observance or lack of observance [of the taboo] is considered of vital importance to the *whole* society involved . . . " (12). Add to this "the root attitude of magic," the "assumption that words are part of the thing to which they refer" (John Condon, qtd. in Oboler 24), the "idea that the name of a thing and its essence have a necessary and invariable relation to each other" (Oboler 24), and one can discover the kinds of assumptions and fears that lend force to even the most contemporary of censorship campaigns, campaigns which otherwise give the appearance of being strictly secular and carefully rational in their concerns and goals.

MacKinnon for example has argued that pornography constitutes a special category not deserving First Amendment protections because the words and images in it are not merely representational symbols: "In pornography, pictures and words are sex" (*Only Words* 26). When she speaks and writes, MacKinnon "reasons" like a believer in voodoo and black magic: she makes no distinction between the representation and what it symbolizes. Words, she has argued, may be "legally treated as the acts they constitute." Thus protecting pornography "means protecting sexual abuse *as* speech" (qtd. in Romano 564 & 563). Playboy, she claims, "takes a woman and makes her sexuality something any man who wants to can . . . hold in his hand for three dollars and fifty cents" (*Feminism* 138). That is some extraordinary feat of magic! If *Playboy* could really do that, the magazine would no doubt cost a lot more than three dollars and fifty cents and would probably be illegal under existing laws dealing with kidnaping or prostitution.

David Mura has written a strong essay in opposition to pornography and has invoked the same now fashionable confusion between symbol and referent. But as he sees it that confusion commonly results from an addiction to pornography: "the addict does not view or read pornography in the same way a scholar might read a poem about shepherds. . . . [T]he addict wants to deny pornography's fictional nature. In refusing the symbolic nature of art, the addict wishes to destroy the indestructible gulf between the sign and its referent" (124-5). By that definition, Catherine MacKinnon would be a pornography addict. For it is she perhaps more than any consumer of pornography who has expressed the wish to destroy the gulf between the sign and its referent: Because of the incorrect "assumption that words have only referential relations to reality, pornography is defended as only words . . . ," when in fact "pornography is an act against women." "In pornography, pictures and words are sex." Pornography constitutes "sexual abuse *as* speech." The group defamation of women which she claims occurs in pornography "is not a mere expression of opinion but a practice of discrimination in verbal form." "The women who are being burned as witches these days are the women in the pornography, and their burning . . . is protected as speech." When you hear a woman screaming from being bounced off the walls by the man she lives with you should understand that "[h]ate speech and pornography do the same thing: enact the abuse" (*Words* 11, 9, 99,104).

MacKinnon even goes so far as to turn it all around. Having defined words as actions, she describes actions as expression. She contends that "[r]ape is expressive. Murder is expressive. . . . That doesn't make [them] protected expression" (*New York Times Magazine*, March 13, 1994). Actually, as we noted above when confronting the misuse of stipulative definitions, MacKinnon saying they are expression doesn't make them expression of any kind, any more than her saying that expression is an assault on women makes it so. Incest does not occur simply because E. Sue Blume stipulates, "Incest can occur through words, sounds, or . . . sights . . . that are sexual but do not involve [the child]" (*Secret Survivors: Uncovering Incest and Its After-Effects in Women,* 5). At least for now, criminal law hasn't capitulated completely to this kind of confusion between symbol and act, although hate speech and hostile sexual environment codes have been greatly influenced by such thinking. MacKinnon contends that, "If . . . representation *is* reality . . . then pornography is no less an act than the rape and torture it represents," and "an audience watching a gang rape in a movie is no different from an audience watching a gang rape" (*Words* 29 & 28). That is a rather big "if." MacKinnon claims that she is not speaking hyperbolically or metaphorically when she speaks of pornography as an act of abuse, but then she will not commit herself to saying that representation is indeed reality. That would be naive indeed and place her with savages and the addicts Mura speaks of who cannot distinguish between representation and reality. It would also place her with psychotics as well.

To say that representation is reality and to assume that readers make no distinction between the two is to reduce all readers to psychotics and to eliminate any distinction between the pleasure of reading and psychotic experience. Based upon current research, Eviatar Zerubavel, a social scientist at Rutgers University, offered this description of psychotics: They seem "to be unaware of the fine lines that keep different experiential realms separate from one another. As a result, they confuse reality with their own dreams and fantasies about it, and *the merely figurative or symbolic with the actual*" (84, my italics). Modern censorship assumes literature to have a power over people which literature does not really posses over ordinary people because it assumes that normal, sane individuals can or do regularly respond to literature no differently from psychotics and cannot discriminate between the symbolic and the actual. If psychotics do respond to literature in that way, censoring literature won't cure them or prevent sociopathic behavior on their part, since there is no telling which literature will set them off. Besides, being psychotic they'll readily confuse their fantasies with any aspect of reality. That is what being psychotic entails.

Of course I don't really believe Mackinon can be placed with psychotics, only that she would have the rest of us viewed as such. In the end she does not truly believe that pornography is the reality it represents. If she truly finds no distinction why hasn't she proposed legislation that would charge pornographers with rape and torture or viewers of it with being accomplices to gang rape? That she hasn't is probably as good proof as any that she does not really believe the inflammatory and deliberately confusing rhetoric she employs, or doesn't believe that it will be accepted beyond the venues where they excite so much enthusiasm. She has proposed civil rights legislation under tort law largely to obviate the First Amendment protections pornography ordinarily enjoys (pornography is protected expression under the U.S. Constitution--a work must be shown to be obscene not be protected). But, despite the now fashionable confusion of word and deed, there is no proposed statute I know of to prosecute pornographers under existing rape or assault law, nor any proposal for trying rapists and murders for violating the First Amendment, even though MacKinnon calls pornography assault and assault expression. Even when the victims have been assassinated to silence them (as Malcolm X or Martin Luther King were), their murderers are not brought up on charges of violating freedom of speech. Rape and murder are indeed not protected by the First Amendment because they are not comprehended by the First Amendment at all--nor any other amendment to the Constitution for that matter. First Amendment law covers expression, and law does not presently adopt the confusion some have perpetrated: It neither treats expression as rape any more than it treats rape as expression. It is not simply that I do not believe that the representation is the reality, and most all people don't either. I don't believe MacKinnon believes it either. It is mere rhetorical hyperbole because she has never proposed in law what she argues in print, that pornographers be arrested for all the "acts" she claims their words and pictures commit.

There is a lot of postmodernist literary and linguistic theory which collapses the distinctions between word and deed, speaks of words as "assaultive," of hate speech as doing violence to minorities, of pornography as rape. These very involved, sophisticated theories which leftist academics are especially fond of, sound suspiciously like the kind of thinking that goes on in what Levi-Strauss, before the age of political correctness, called "the savage mind." And indeed they have fostered repression in thought and word for similar superstitious reasons. As Wendy Steiner puts it, "leftist literalists operate with an utterly naive conception of art as magic, directly efficacious in reality and requiring stringent regulation if society is to be 'protected'" (82).

MacKinnon has complained of "the First Amendment bog, the distinction between speech and conduct" (*Feminism* 208). But what she calls a bog is the very cast of mind which has served to liberate human thought and the civilization it made possible from superstitious and mythic modes of thinking. Admittedly Western civilization has not treated women well, although women fair far better in modern Western civilization than in any civilization we know of. But if no civilization has treated women well it is not for getting bogged down in the distinction between words and deeds. Those who hanged and burned witches made little distinction between the curses they claimed the women uttered and the evil it supposedly caused. In Massachusetts, the execution of witches counted on what was called "spectral evidence"--the testimony of witnesses that the spectre of the accused witch visited and harmed them and their families and livestock. These witnesses would scream and writhe in court, claiming the spectre was attacking them, and such testimony was taken for true. Common sense triumphed over empirical evidence, even though no person in the court could perceive the presence or action of the supposed spectre. Cotton Mather noted how "the *Spectres* have an odd faculty of clothing the most substantial and corporeal Instruments of Torture, with Invisibility . . . wholly unseen to the standers by . . . ." He found in all of witchcraft nothing "more Unaccountable , than the trick which the Witches have to render themselves, and their Tools *Invisible"* (69, 131). But within about a year's time the people of Massacheussets came to their senses and the courts ruled that conviction on the basis of spectral evidence was unlawful. "Deprived of such evidence . . . there was noting left, nothing tangible, nothing provable" (Starkey 242).

If we are to believe present day witchunters, obscene material possesses the same odd and unaccountable ability to clothe both the agency by which it works and the effects it produces with invisibility. Our own witchunters continue to accept spectral evidence of harm, evidence which is utterly intangible, immeasurable and unprovable, and to dismiss scientific evidence which shows that no tangible or provable evidence of harm exists. And for two centuries modern courts have yet to do what the Puritan fathers in Massachuessets did: rule that such spectral evidence be inadmissible. People continue to be convicted even though nothing tangible and nothing provable can be presented to show that they harm anyone. They continue to be convicted because the law having recognized that nothing tangible can be presented has repeatedly ruled that no tangible proof of harm is required to convict!

Our ability to understand and manipulate symbols in a free abstract manner divorced from the actions and things they symbolize is one of the very characteristics that distinguishes not only the civilized from the savage mind (whether the latter lives on a jungle plateau or a university campus), but *homo sapiens* from other species. The mentality of a dog is bogged down in its *inability* to distinguish words from conduct. It will respond to "fetch," or "sit," or "come here," with the appropriate action, but if you try and hold a conversation with such an animal and tell it, "I want you to sit when I stop talking," it will most likely just wag its tail, happily unable to decipher any meaning other than that it is being given attention by its mistress. Not coincidentally, MacKinnon ignores millions of years of evolutionary advantage and assigns to human beings (especially of the male gender) a mental agility not much better than a dog's. Just as a dog springs into action upon hearing the word "fetch", so does the stimulus of obscene material by-pass the enlarged cerebral cortex built up by hundreds of millions of years of evolution, and humans are said to respond to obscenity by suddenly losing the ability to think abstractly and distinguish word from deed, symbol from thing, fiction from fact, and stripped of all voluntary conscious decision-making operations, the person will spring into action at the "command" of obscene material: she will commit acts of adultery (as people in the nineteenth century thought), he will be driven to delinquency (as the 1950's led us to believe), or violence and rape (as some contemporary feminists contend). Once again obscene literature supposedly acts in a way different from other forms of literature. Others may give us pause to think, may enrich our minds or move us emotionally, or give us pleasure. Obscene literature may do some or all of that as well, but for the censors, it overwhelmingly operates on our minds like a stimulus-response reflex action: it moves us to act like "fetch" moves a dog: *"Saying* 'kill' to a trained dog is only words. Yet it is . . . seen as performing an act tantamount to someone's destruction, like saying 'ready, aim, fire' to a firing squad." Likewise,"the message of these [pornographic] materials . . . is 'get her,' pointing to all women . . . . This message is addressed directly to the penis, delivered through an erection, and taken out on women in the real world" (*Words* 12 & 21).

In what has become a favorite catch phrase of the anti-porn feminists, Robin Morgan said, "Pornography is the theory, rape is the practice." The problem is not only that everyone knows darn well what the usual practice is: It is masturbation. The problem is that Robin Morgan also knows not to get bogged down in any distinction between word and the deed represented. Pornography, like any literature, says a lot of different things to a lot of different people. There is not one message to any work of art or literature however blunt and crude a work it may be. It is not simply that Morgan or MacKinnon say pornography says only or primarily one thing, it is that they would have us believe that what they say it says acts as effectively upon a man as "fetch" or "kill" does upon a dog. Pornography can of course *naturally* excite certain physiological responses in *healthy* individuals. It stimulates the cardio-vascular system, the adrenal gland, and yes, the penis, but these are all *involuntary* responses, whereas the actions which may or may not result from them, such as masturbation, rape, or love-making, are anything but immediate and involuntary. They do not follow automatically in the way an erection may follow the sight of a beautiful woman or a well-built man, but require a sequence of conscious decisions. The human brain and nervous system being what they are, neither pornography nor any work of art or literature sends its message directly to the voluntary motor system. Obscenity stimulates no practice in humans! And even the penis is more discriminating than MacKinnon allows. It is not interested in "getting" all women. All men find that many women send no message whatsoever to their sex glands.

Legend has it that in ancient Greece Zeuxis could paint grapes so real that the birds would peck at them. Goethe observed that this proved not that they were real grapes, but real birds. Painted grapes may have the power to fool birds, but Goethe understood what few censors do, that humans have the capacity not to be fooled by representations. Unlike those of other species our neuro-motor system is simply not constituted in such a way that we cannot practically distinguish between pictures of grapes or representations of men and women from the real things. (Besides there is little evidence that birds or dogs also don't know the difference. Actually birds won't peck at painted grapes, though, as reported in *Discover* magazine, Japanese scientists have recently trained pigeons to distinguish between pictures of Picasso and Monet. If the picture of a plucked chicken, bound and hanging on the wall, would drive roosters to rape and violence, then I might consider changing my position. But there's no evidence for that behavior either.)

We all also understand language and the context from which messages reach us well enough to easily recognize the difference which MacKninnon ignores between language uttered as a command and as an expression. Even if the message of pornography was 'get her' that does not constitute a command and neither the brain nor the penis understands it as such. Every sane individual understands the difference between the expression "I think all women ought to be shot" and the command "I want you to get a gun and shoot every woman you see."

That is a difference the censor does not allow because the logic of so much censorship when it describes expression as a potent force for harm depends upon the reification of language. With great fervor, the speaker finds himself "really talking about filth" and believes in his enthusiasm that is the same as talking about "real filth," and he would have everyone else make the same mistake.   Christie Davies has collected several examples from British parliamentary debates:

> There never was such a time when there was so much concern about clean air and clean food . . . . [W]e have not shown the same sort of concern about clean books . . . . [D]irty air and dirty food can poison the bodies of men and women but dirty books poison the soul which is an infinitely more serious matter.

> This Bill must be sufficiently armed to deal with mere pornography . . . , just as our public health law is properly armed to deal with the discharge of untreated sewage in public and for the same reason, except that in one case we are concerned with the physical health and in the other with the moral and mental health.

> The purpose of this legislation is to give a power to destroy obscene matter before it can do harm, . . . a power more akin to the removal of refuse from the

streets that to the ordinary criminal procedure.

No responsible authority could agree that a right to such freedom [from censorship] can belong to any man. Any more than any man has the right to freedom to go around poisoning the public water supply.

The fountainhead of our national life should not be polluted at its source. (28)

Alexander M. Bickel in a *Reader's Digest* interview (February, 1974) assured us, "Societies polluted by moral stench are not likely to survive." But perhaps the most famous comparison came from Jack Douglas writing in *The Sunday Express* (1928): "I would rather put a phial of prussic acid in the hand of a healthy boy or girl than the book in question." We have listened to this foolishness for so long, have accepted the suppression of all kinds of literature based upon these absurd comparisons for centuries now that few even think to question how absurd they actually are. Either the people who draw them do not literally believe what they say and there is no reason to take seriously the dangers they cite, or else they do take it literally or would at least have everyone else do it, and then not only is their logic utterly absurd, but they themselves pose a serious threat. Aldous Huxley made just that point: "I offered to provide Mr. Douglas with a child, a bottle of prussic acid, a copy of *The Well of Loneliness* [the book in question], and (if he kept his word and chose to administer the acid) a handsome memorial in marble to be erected wherever he might appoint, after his execution. The offer, I regret to say, was not accepted." (qtd. in Kendrick 258-9). Carlin Romano writing in *The Nation* (November 15, 1993) tried the same tactic. He took MacKinnon at her word that she understood no real difference between being raped and being exposed to pornography and proposed that he decide to rape her before writing a review of her book. True to her word, MacKinnon said of the review that she felt she had been publicly raped--proof perhaps that MacKinnon, who claims to speak for all women, does not know what it is to be publicly raped. No sensible, sane, and reasonable person, if given the choice, would say she finds no difference whether she is verbally attacked in a publication or raped in a public setting. Most all of us do make a clear distinction between offence and harm.

Were I to eat a *Hustler* centerfold, such "filth" would have no more ill effect on me than if I ingested St. Paul's Epistles (provided I spit out the staples), and a lot less than if I ate untreated sewage; and if everyone in American society were to breathe dirty air and eat dirty food none of us would likely survive, but not one society has died as a result of the intake of "moral stench." As Ortega y Gasset remarked, "I do not recollect that any civilization ever perished from an attack of doubt" (reported in *New York Times*, July 3, 1949), and the same may be said for attacks of "moral pollution." American and European societies have survived for centuries amidst continual moral change, some perhaps for the better, some, according to others, for the worse. They may survive in a different form, but no society dies from changes in moral outlook, so long, that is, as we do not believe, as many who would censor do, that the basis and purpose of a society is to realize and preserve certain ideological systems of thought (more about that in the next section).

Modern censorship is no more modern for not invoking fear of the devil, since it survives on the same kind of superstitious reasoning which ascribes diabolical agency to whatever one fears or dislikes. But there remains one more antiquated explanation for the harms expression supposedly causes. It goes by the name of "degeneracy theory," and historically it was in its own day an attempt to modernize the even then superstitious belief in demon possession.

We have already noted how obscenity law in modern secular societies involved the transfer to the common law courts of what had formerly been religious offences reserved for the ecclesiastical courts. This occurred in the eighteenth century, and not coincidentally, also in "the eighteenth century demon-possession theory was replaced by degeneracy theory" which "was used to explain both individual and social ills" by attributing "the cause of [mental, physical and moral] degeneracy . . . to loss of vital fluid in masturbation, or promiscuity, and also to indulgence in concupiscent thoughts and fantasies" (Money 450-1). In *Frauds Exposed* (1880), Comstok used the theory to explain the extensive evils obscene publications were capable of generating. The effect of the "cursed business" was to breed lust, and lust

> defiles the body, debauches the imagination, corrupts the mind, deadens the will, destroys the memory, sears the conscience, hardens the heart, and damns the soul. It unnerves the arm, and steals away the elastic step. It robs the soul of manly virtues . . . . The family is polluted [by the traffic in obscene publications], home desecrated, and each generation born into the world is more and more cursed by the inherited weaknesses, the harvest of this seed-sowing of the Evil one.

Added to this was the unfounded and later medically disproved assumption that sexual variations were socially contagious. With the advent of germ theory in the 1870's, we came to understand how diseases are contracted by individuals and how they are transmitted throughout society, and degeneracy and contagion theories were abandoned in all branches of medicine. All that is but one: In sexology, these outmoded theories are "still resorted to as an explanation of why explicit depictions of erotic sexuality . . . are dangerous to the individual and society" (Money 449-51). It is still believed *contrary to all clinical evidence* that a person's sexual make-up, orientation, and desires may be fundamentally altered simply by coming into contact with depictions of different sexual practices, that persons, for example, who have no homo-erotic desires or with no interest in bondage can be "infected" with these desires, can be turned on to them simply by viewing or reading about them.

Believing that variant sexual interests and practices were inevitably and necessarily symptomatic of disease, that they were filthy and sick, it was simple enough to believe that erotic material was the pollution that caused the disease. But variations in sexual desire are no necessary indicators of disease, and even if abnormal sexual interest were a disease, we now know full well how disease is contracted and transmitted throughout society, and we know for certain that it is not gotten by reading. If lesbianism were a contagious or infectious disease one could not contract lesbianism by reading *The Well of Loneliness* any more than one could come down with tuberculosis by reading *The Magic Mountain,* or AIDS by subscribing to *The New England Journal of Medicine.* As literature is not the agency of the devil so is it not the carrier of disease. Those who ascribe this special power to literature are only offering a modernized version of demon possession theories, but one that is equally at odds with sound reasoning and everything that science tells us. The truth of the matter, contrary to what modern censorship campaigns repeatedly would have us believe, is that the "fantasies of paraphilia . . . are not preferences borrowed from movies, books, or other people. . . . Paraphilic fantasies and behavior are not caused by social contagion. A person [for example] who does not have klismaphilia can look at five, fifty, or five hundred enema movies of someone getting erotically and genitally turned on by getting an enema, and never be able to get turned on that way himself or herself. Klismaphilic movies are a turn-on only for people who have klismaphilia" (Money 449-50). And as I suggested earlier, I would expect that every reader knows this from his or her own experience. If one were to recall his or own earliest, pre-pubescent sexual predilections, pre-occupations and fantasies, I think most everyone would agree that they are the same as the predilections, pre-occupations, and fantasies one has had throughout his or her adult life. How we got them, neither we nor anyone else knows, but we certainly didn't choose them--

though we may have discovered them one day or night when some dream or image of a man or woman, or a man and a man or a woman and a woman struck us as exceptionally interesting and exciting.

In examining the issue of harm, what it all goes back to is this: long before post-modernist theories blurred the distinction between word and deed for the purpose of censoring expression, the Attorney General of Britain did just that. He inaugurated the modern approach to censoring expression as a criminal offence in secular society by contending that "the peace may be broken without an actual force," that "to corrupt the morals of the King's subjects is against the peace of the King." Thus it has been for over two hundred and fifty years that words and images have been held to break the peace without the use of actual force: What that peace-breaking force is which words and images have, if it is not actual force, no one has seen, no one can find, no one has measured, and no one really has to. Since the early eighteenth century, the law has repeatedly said that one does not have to present evidence of actual force or find evidence of actual harm in order to censor expression. Consequently in modern secular societies, words are understood to be distinguishable from deeds *except when they run contrary to conventional morality.* The words or images that depict what is immoral are presumed to have the power to break the peace.

And what it all boils down to is this: All attempts to legislate morality by regulating speech have redefined harm, offered stipulative definitions of what constitutes violations to persons or society, conflated speech with action, image with the thing represented, offered all levels of difficult, and confusing, literary, philosophical, rhetorical, aesthetic, linguistic and legal theories for one simple reason: Neither they nor anyone else has ever been able to demonstrate that expression produces observable or measurable harm! There has never been evidence sufficient enough to convince people of the need to regulate expression for the reason that it may cause actual harm.

Louis B. Schwartz summed up the extraordinary nature of modern morals offences like obscenity quite succinctly when he wrote:

> What truly distinguishes offenses commonly thought of as 'against morals' is not their relation to morality but the absence of ordinary justification for punishment in a non-theocratic state. The ordinary justification for secular penal controls is preservation of public order. Individuals must be able to go about their lawful pursuits without fear of attack, plunder, or other harm. No such results impend from the commission of 'morals offenses.' What the

dominant lawmaking groups appear to be seeking by means of morals legislation is not security and freedom in their own affairs but restraint of conduct by others that is regarded as offensive. (86)

But what one might also note with respect to modern morals offences is that "the only kind of immorality toward which all this is directed is sexual immorality. Nothing has ever been censored on the ground that it had a tendency to promote dishonesty or cruelty or cowardice. No significant legislative attempt has ever been made to suppress books except to preserve the political order, the established piety or theoretical standards of sexual behavior" (Rembar 21). As Rembar has noted, some have recently called for censorship of violent matter, but twenty-eight years after Rembar wrote there is still no significant legislative attempt to do so. There has been in the intervening years significant and successful attempts to outlaw pornography on the ground that it encourages violence against women, but significantly, the mostly women who have voiced those concerns about violence against women have tended to focus upon X-rated pornography and to ignore almost entirely the R-rated films and videos where, in large numbers of action, horror and slasher films, extreme and graphic violence committed against women is not an uncommon feature.

The revealing fact is that those who claim expression harms modern society almost invariably attribute the harms to sexual expression of some kind and ignore all other types, even the most violent, brutal and abusive; and the modern feminist critique of pornography remains no exception. Thus most all modern censors attribute to erotic literature a power to move us different from all other literature, but moreover, their relative lack of interest in nonsexual forms of criminal, immoral or pathological behavior can be measured by the fact that few modern censors hold that murder, lying, or depression result from reading the wrong things. Depression, the most common form of mental disorder, is not believed to result from the many sad and tragic works of literature we encounter. Nor do we claim that any work of literature sent its message directly to the trigger finger of a murderer in the way that saying "kill" speaks to a trained dog.

Every society seeks to censor what it finds most threatening. In the past it was blasphemous utterances directed against God and the Church or seditious libel directed against monarchs and noblemen, and for modern bourgeois society the greatest threat to its moral foundations has been seen to lie primarily with sexual liberty and that is therefore what it invariably seeks to control. This transition from ancient to modern concerns can perhaps best be seen in a report one police official wrote in 1797 respecting the advisability of seizing copies of Sade's *Justine*. The lower orders resented the libertinism of their superiors and so when the modern bourgeois state began to emerge, it would regard the licentiousness which had characterized the behavior of the nobility in the past as tantamount to what the nobility of the *ancien regime* once feared, attacks upon the government and government officials: "I place licentious works such as the one I am denouncing to the authorities [*Justine*]," one police inspector said, "in the same class as attack upon the government, because if courage founds republics, good morals preserve them. Their ruin almost always leads to the fall of empires" (see Lever 499).

To justify censorship for the stated purpose of securing individuals from harm is a bogus claim not only for the reason that there is no evidence that expression can produce actual harm, but because it is not to protect individuals from harm that judges, or preachers, or feminists seek to censor. What they seek is to protect from attack the particular moral system they value and which perhaps is the basis of their power and authority. It is the harm which expression can do to ideas which censorship guards against. Just what kind of ideas require such protection is our next subject of discussion.

Chapter 5

Why Opinions Are Censored

Censor was the name given to the Roman magistrates who took the census of the citizens, and among their duties which Cicero describes in *The Laws* was that "they shall regulate the morals of the people." Censorship most usually involves government regulation of moral opinion and thereby presumably the morality of the conduct which stems from it. It arises, as Jefferson noted, when men set up "their own opinions . . . as the only true and infallible, and as such [endeavor] to impose them on others" ("Bill for Establishing Religious Freedom").

But why is it necessary to enforce opinion? What is it about opinions that makes them so susceptible to censorship? There are all kinds of obvious reasons that men have given down through the ages having to do with important matters of truth, or divine command, or the maintenance of moral order and social stability. But I would suggest something more fundamental, something basic to the nature of opinions and beliefs themselves which, whatever their subject matter may be, has tended to make their imposition or their suppression a common practice: It is that, as we know, opinions tend to vary. Moreover, the acceptance or rejection of any opinion tends to vary from one person or group to another because it is in the very nature of opinion to vary: Whatever it may be about, *an opinion cannot be convincingly communicated as knowledge from one person or group of believers to another.*

We know that bodies in a vacuum accelerate at a rate of thirty-two feet per second per second, and insofar as that fact can be demonstrated anywhere in the world, it can be communicated as knowledge to anyone in the world, irrespective of that person's gender, religion, class or nationality. But there is no reliable way of demonstrating to those who hold opinions different from one's own that one's own opinions are true or that theirs are false. Men have therefore repeatedly resorted to censorship, to the repression and enforcement of opinion for the reason that, given the nature of opinion and belief, there was no possible way they could reasonably demonstrate the supposed truth of their beliefs to those who did not already accept them as true. As we shall see, men have imposed their opinions on others, often by the most violent of means, not simply because they have mistaken their opinions for the only true ones, but basically because they have mistaken opinion for truth in the first place.

In ancient China, one of the founders of Taoism, was the first significant thinker to understand that opinions are characteristically taken for the truth by the people who hold them (that's it) and taken not to be true by those who hold other positions (that's not): the world, Chuang-tzu observed, "has no common 'it' for 'that's it', and each of us treats as 'it' what is 'it' for him." What "is it for one of them [the followers of Confucius or Mo-tzu] for the others is not, and what is not for one of them for the other is" (Graham 101, 52). What is more, since the perceived truth or falsity of an opinion varies with changes in persons' viewpoints, the nature of opinion is such that the opinions anyone holds to be true cannot be communicated as knowledge to those holding positions different from one's own. Thus the famous statement which appears in both Chuang-tzu and Lao-tzu, the two originators of Taoist thought: "The Way [the Tao] is incommunicable."

In the ancient Western world, the founder of Christian faith, came to the exact same conclusion about the nature of his beliefs. Paul recognized that belief was not something men could agree upon and that the nature of faith was such that one could not possibly communicate it to others in such a way that they might thereby come to recognize it as anything other than absurd: "my speech and my message," he said, "are not in plausible words of wisdom," but "a secret and hidden wisdom," that "is veiled," and generally appears to be "foolish" (1 *Cor.* 2.4-5; 1*Cor.* 2.7; 2 *Cor.* 4.3;, 1 *Cor* 1.23).

But this is where the similarities end. For where Chuang-tzu and Paul both recognized the various and irreconcilable nature of opinion and belief, Chuang-tzu insisted that, "Heaven is impartial to everything it covers" (Graham 93), but Paul's Heaven was not impartial. Paul insisted that, even though his opinions were at that time restricted to a small band of believers and were not shared by almost everyone else, that they were still in the nature of truth. Indeed Paul mistook his opinions for the highest truths of all! And mistaking opinion for truth he mistakenly invested truth with characteristics which were and are peculiar to opinion: he described truth as being just like opinion, as being by its very nature relative and incommunicable. This mistake would change for close to two thousand years what Western civilization would continue to understand the nature of truth to be. Thus for example in the twentieth century Leopold Averbakh, a leading Soviet literary figure, could recognize, similar to Paul and just about everyone else for that matter, that values tend to vary from one group to another. As Nadezhda Mandelstam noted about him, "nothing was absolute and all values were conditioned by class," but that did not prevent him, like Paul and so many others, from elevating his particular values to universal truths. He was "not at all put out by the fact that his own class values were now regarded as absolutes" (164).

This mistaking of opinion for truth (which as we shall see did not originate with Paul) would have far-reaching and devastating consequences. For once men mistook their particular beliefs for truth and thereby transformed the truth as they understood it into something relative and incommunicable, they then had to confront two basic problems of their own creation: 1) Why is it that almost everyone else does not accept what I understand to be the truth? and 2) how can I make truth generally accepted if when I speak it my words appear to the people who do not possess the truth to be foolish and implausible? The explanation they gave and the solutions they proposed would be used throughout Western history to justify censorship, repression, and bloodshed.

We speak of relativists versus absolutists as if what distinguishes them is their differing views on the nature of truth, the former supposedly doubting that we can know or agree upon the truth, the latter convinced of the existence of eternal verities. However, the disagreement here does not usually involve different attitudes toward truth, but toward opinion and belief. Indeed, when it is a question of the phenomenology of opinion, there seems to be no real disagreement between them that men's opinions respecting what is true do indeed tend to vary. So what truly distinguishes the relativist from the absolutist is the different ways in which each believes one ought to respond to this obvious, readily observable fact--whether the person recognizes his opinion as one among many or elevates it above all others as an absolute truth which others are wrong for not accepting. The difference is not merely one for philosophic debate. For if one believes, as many absolutists are prone to, that all humankind will ultimately somehow be required to accept their opinion as the only true one, they often then tend to appoint themselves and their henchmen as enforcers of their truth.

Paul's explanation as to why others did not accept what he took to be true is the one that has been given by believers of most all faiths, whether religious or secular, down through the ages. For such people, the problem is usually not seen to lie with one's own understanding (that perhaps one's beliefs are not matters of eternal, absolute, or universal truth after all). Nor is it thought to lie with the methods of persuasion and communication one employs or fails to employ (that maybe one has failed to offer evidence or demonstrable proofs sufficient to gain voluntary general agreement). No, the problem is that there is something wrong with those who refuse to see the truth: The "minds of the unbelievers," Paul contended, are "blinded"; they "believe what is false" (2 *Cor.* 4.4; 2 *Thess.* 2.11). This shifting of responsibility from the speaker who cannot convincingly demonstrate the truth of his opinions to those who do not therefore accept them as true has served down through the centuries to establish a hierarchy of belief. It allows the believer to see humanity not as distinguished by the variety of different beliefs and opinions men hold, but by the supposed fact that a select and superior few know the truth, by virtue of the special gifts they have been graced with, and everyone else does not, due to some flaw within their character, either because we are born with original sin, or are blinded by class, race or gender bias, or remain morally and intellectually deficient. According to Paul's version, there are those "who posses the Spirit" and those who do "not receive the gifts of the Spirit of God, for they are folly to [them], and [they are] not able to understand them" (I *Cor.* 2.12-14). According to Lord Cockburn and other judges both on the bench and off, there are those who by their literary preferences reveal not differences in taste, but minds open to "immoral influences." To such ways of thinking, differences of opinion (or belief or taste) do not demonstrate the variable nature of opinion itself, but rather, on the basis of the opinions persons hold, they presumably reveal themselves to others to be saints or sinners destined for heaven or hell, virtuous or corrupt and deserving to be praised or pilloried, wise or depraved and deserving to be listened to or locked up.

Paul was a highly educated Roman citizen, familiar with the philosophy of his day, and his distinction between the spiritually gifted men who know the truth and the naturally gifted who do not runs along the same line Plato drew to distinguish the few from the many: "true opinion [regarding the physical world] is a faculty . . . shared by all men, intelligence [regarding things not seen] by the gods and only a small number of men" (*Timeus* 70). It also shares with Plato's thought the belief that truth cannot be generally communicated to the many beyond the aristocratic few who accept it. Men, Plato insisted, "who have no natural affinity [with] forms of excellence cannot acquire such knowledge as is attainable about virtue and vice"

(*Letters* 140).   Likewise, Paul contended that what he called wisdom was designed by God not to bring men together, but for the very purpose of creating distinctions among them: "not many of you were wise according to worldly standards . . . ; but God chose what is foolish in the world to shame the wise" (I *Cor.* 1.26-7).

"Philosophy had been an aristocratic movement from its very inception" and as such "had been recognized as dangerous to democratic principles . . ." (Ferguson 104). But before Plato and other philosophers redefined it, the conception of truth among the scientists and democrats of ancient Greece was not of something which served to create divisions and distinctions among men. Truth, they believed, was something which could be taught and learned, which could bring men together, and which is finally something which they can share in common. Before Plato changed thinking for about seventeen-hundred years it was generally believed that men "act reasonably in accepting the advice of a smith and shoemaker in political matters" and that "virtue can be taught [to] and cultivated [by]" any person (*Protagoras* 56), and men sought in free and open debate to deal only with "matters known to the general public" (*On Ancient Medicine* 71). The conception of truth which Plato formulated in reaction to the democratic thinking of his day and which Paul later adopted as the basis of Christian faith involved mistaking the personal opinions and beliefs of a select class of people for general, universal, eternal truth, and as a result, what they mistook for general truth seemed generally incapable of being communicated by means of reasonable persuasion to the many who, because they disagreed with the opinions of a few, were therefore seen to be immune to reasonable persuasion.

Hannah Arendt has noted that Plato's "whole political philosophy, including his outspoken tyrannical traits, rests on the conviction that truth [cannot be] communicated to the many" (235). We might note that *most all censorship is based precisely upon the mistaken conviction that truth cannot be communicated to the many*. It is mistaken, first of all, because truth unlike the beliefs which pass for it can indeed be communicated to many different peoples. So the problem is not, as Plato or Paul assumed, that the highest truths are incommunicable because most people are generally unreceptive to them. The problem is that most people are unreceptive because thinkers from ancient to modern times are not dealing with truth of any kind: most all censorship results from the fact that a few people come to cherish their particular opinions or beliefs so strongly and deeply that they presume them to constitute universal truths. What they discover is that their beliefs when presented to the world as though they were truths in fact do not behave like truths, and they place the blame for this upon the many who, in their opinion, cannot accept the truth. (In modern democracies that assessment has changed in keeping with democratic thinking: it is now held that truth cannot be communicated to the few who are morally deficient, though the courts have repeatedly ruled that those few nevertheless determine what everyone else will not be permitted to read.)

To this day the justification for censorship continues to derive from this peculiar conception of truth as exclusive and incommunicable. Such a re-thinking of the nature of truth was first formulated in antiquity by aristocratic philosophers reacting to the democratic conception of truth as something comprehensive and inclusive, as that which involved common knowledge that ultimately brought all reasonable people together, regardless of rank or class.   The legacy these ancient aristocrats bequeathed to Western civilization was a definition of truth that was divisive, hierarchic, anti-democratic, and anti-egalitarian. Opinion disguised and presented as truth served to divide men for centuries into superior and inferior classes and to justify all kinds of censorship and repression.

But if others did not understand the truth because of their supposedly inherent inferiority, how then bring the ignorant many with whom the select few could not reason to agree with what the few understood to be true? In the first book of *The Republic,* Thrasymachus, not won over by Socrates' words, is asked to explain his position further: "And how am I to convince you, he said, if you are not already convinced by what I have just said?" Scientists and democrats from Socrates' day had already offered an answer to such questions: opinions need to be publicized widely, demonstrable proofs that can be commonly understood need to be presented, and through open dialogue and debate the views of others have to be taken into account. If this all sounds familiar, it ought to be. It is the same response modern republicans and democrats like Milton, Jefferson, or Mill presented to the threat of censorship in modern time, and it represents a tradition, though not as continuous, which is in fact older than the aristocratic-philosophic position that replaced it. But Plato, perhaps the first great architect of totalitarian rule in the West, answered Thrasymachus' question in works like *The Republic* and *The Laws* with proposals for the   legal repression of contrary opinion.   It is the answer tyrants have been giving for over two thousand years.

Thrasymachus' question has reverberated with horrible consequences down through history. Mao, who also mistook his beliefs for the truth, was still asking it in 1962: "What should we do if we persuade [the people] and they are not convinced?" And he was answering it in the same way: "a few people," he estimated, "have to be arrested and executed . . ." (183-4). And before him Augustine, recognizing what Paul had said from the first, that "words," "arguments," and "reason," cannot achieve "unity in Christ," accepted the use of force whereby through "fear of suffering, and dread of those laws in promulgation of which kings serve the Lord," men could be "compelled to examine the truth" (203, 205). In 1965 Lord Devlin, like Augustine, recognized that morality was maintained by two instruments: "The two instruments are those of teaching, which is doctrine [specifically Christian doctrine], and of enforcement, which is law." And he too recognized that teaching alone was insufficient and therefore enforcement was necessary to maintain any moral doctrine within society, since "after centuries of debate, men of undoubted reasoning power and honesty of purpose have shown themselves unable to agree upon what the moral law should be, differing sometimes upon the answer to the simplest moral problem" (25 & 93).

It is one of the great and curious ironies that censors, assured of the truth of their opinions, repeatedly attack the evils of relativism and skepticism when in fact they are the ones who resort to enforcement precisely because it is they who despair of "reason" and "honesty of purpose" ever reconciling the disparate views men hold. They would have us believe that skepticism and relativism with regard to truth is an evil by-product of the modern scientific age when in fact the relativism they lament and seek to eliminate, often by force, is not a characteristic of scientific knowledge nor original to modernity. Ancient Eastern and Western civilizations have well documented for us in the writings of the sophists or the Taoists or even those who opposed them that the nature of human societies has always been such that men within them have different and irreconcilable opinions--and Herodotus for one was perhaps the first to show how opinions differed even more severely between men of different societies and cultures. That in and of itself does not make truth relative, but only shows that opinions are. It is only when men began to mistake their various opinions for the Way or the Truth or the Life that truth came to be understood as relative, since men never agreed on the true way, and could not be gotten to agree or at least say they agree without the use of force. As a result more than a few men have had to be executed in Mao's China and elsewhere throughout this world of ours because it has always been the case that the overwhelming many have never accepted the opinions of the few: the overwhelming majority in the world are not Platonists or Maoists or Muslims or Christians or Jews or adherents of any other system of belief one would care to name. Thus it has all too often been true that the few who hold power have found it expedient to keep arresting and killing everyone who disagreed with them--an endless task which they find preferable to admitting that their beliefs may not be true.

The difference between a skeptic and an absolutist is, as we have suggested, not simply or so much that the one holds truth to be relative while the other takes it to be universal. The difference hasn't to do with differing views on the nature of truth itself, but with the reasons given as to why people might not understand it. The difference is that the skeptic believes we can never agree on the truth because truth, whatever he takes it to be, lies beyond *all* human comprehension. However, the absolutist believes we can't get at what he is sure he knows to be the truth because everyone who disagrees with him is too corrupt or stupid to understand it. Both of course are wrong (because they are describing belief not truth), but skeptics do not have a history of executing those who disagree with them. No skeptic has ever arrested or executed people or sent his subjects to war because men have not doubted enough. The extensive, measurable harms done to people throughout Western history cannot be attributed to the unbelievers in any society. And recent books have it all wrong which suggest that skepticism and maybe even a loss of belief in the devil have left us with no way of explaining to ourselves the evil that pervades society. When all is said and done devilworshippers account for little evil in the world. If we would seek for an explanation for one great evil that has pervaded human history we haven't far to look. We could start with the Bible. It tells us what would remain a sorry fact of Western history till the present day, that more people have been slaughtered in the name of God than the devil. Persistent evil on a worldwide scale is usually the result of men fighting for goodness and truth and not evil and the devil.

Scientific thinking so far from producing relativism has for the first time in recorded history established truth on a universal basis insofar as everyone regardless of religion, class, or country accepts the same scientific principles. And what is perhaps its greatest achievement is that scientific knowledge, unlike religious or philosophic opinion, has succeeded in gaining literally worldwide acceptance without the use of force. Scientific truth is the same in Singapore as it is in Souix City. Indeed science remains the *only* method ever invented by human ingenuity to achieve what all other endeavors have attempted and failed to accomplish: It has established its truths as universally true, and perhaps what is even more significant, it has done so without violence. The same cannot be said for the so-called truths of religion or philosophy or morality.

Admittedly, as hear over and again, mostly from critics of science, there are many questions science cannot answer. We are usually reminded that what are taken to be the most important questions science especially fails to answer. Questions like: What is the meaning of life? Is life worth living? Is there a God, and if so, why won't He leave us alone already? It is thereby strongly implied, if not stated directly, that we must turn elsewhere for the answers. By why single out science for special indictment? The fact of the matter is that science cannot answer these questions because no human effort has ever been able to come up with generally satisfying answers to them. Why else are we still asking them? The nature of the great questions--and one major reason they persist in intriguing us--is that they cannot be answered. If they could be answered, they would not only not be great questions, they wouldn't even be questions of any kind any longer. So one can just as accurately say: Religion is incapable of answering the great questions, or philosophy, or morality . . .

Neither science, nor religion, nor the lived life of human experience, can answer the important questions. The significant difference when it comes to science lies in the way science goes about answering the questions that can be answered and in the fact that it does not invent answers to questions that admit of no generally accepted answer. After all, the imposition of invented answers to unanswerable questions remains a moving force behind much censorship and repression.

We also need to recall that those in authority would likely lose their authority over us not only if they admitted they could not answer life's mysteries, but if they actually posed questions that could be answered and then answered them. Why come back on Friday, Saturday, or Sunday to find the answer to a question which was resolved the week before? If you speak in riddles and offer nonsense many, if not most will think you profound for the very reason that they cannot fathom what you are saying and will not hesitate coming back again and again to discover what you really mean.

As one modern scientists has noted, "the most socially and culturally distinguishing feature of science" is that its "propositions can be verified by any competent person irrespective of their social, religious, or political views; they are by design intended to be true for everyone" (Pagels 172, 210). The so-called truths of philosophy and religion, as Plato, Paul and others have noted, are not designed to be true for everyone. Even in ancient times men who rebelled against the methods of philosophy understood that the philosopher's conception of truth meant that "a man might know the truth . . . without either he or his audience being able to judge whether it were the truth or not, because there is no sure criterion" (*Hippocratic Writings* 70). These different understandings of and approaches to the truth explain why in both ancient and modern times, science and democracy have tended to appear together and why, as Francois Jacob noted, "no genocide has yet been committed for the triumph of a scientific theory" (Jacob x): Scientists, unlike philosophers, can offer demonstrable proof for their propositions, and such proofs are essential if one is ever going to achieve a voluntary consensus of agreement as to what is true.

The same cannot be said for the triumph of beliefs because "the characteristic of a belief is precisely that it is not regarded as knowledge by those who do not share it." Any so-called philosophic or religious "wisdom . . . must distinguish if it is prudent, between the taking up of personal positions and those of restricted groups, relative to beliefs that are self-evident for some but not shared by others, and demonstrable truths open to everyone" (Piaget 228, 210). But such prudence has been the exception rather than the guiding principle when it comes to the moral, political, and religious beliefs men hold. Beliefs and opinions do not travel well. They are not open to everyone because they can offer no demonstrable proofs of their truthfulness and thus can never be generally accepted by persuasion alone. Without societal or government enforcement, without censorship, coercion and outright violence, opinions have never been and indeed can never be generally accepted as true. And when such enforcement is in effect, "acceptance," as I suggested earlier, amounts merely to orthodoxy and not necessarily belief. Orthodoxy (which, we recall, means correct opinion) is all any institution of authority requires to maintain itself. So long as everyone publicly gives lip-service to the true faith or the party line it does not matter what people truly believe. The rapidity with which the Soviet Union collapsed suggests how little all those Marxist-Leninist citizens actually believed the opinions they had been forced to give expression to. The reason why various religious institutions have maintained themselves for thousands of years is not that they do indeed embody the truth. The reason is that there never can be any evidence to prove or, what is more significant, to disprove the transcendent truths they claim as the basis of their authority. In this world there can therefore be no evidence to refute their fundamental beliefs about God, or Heaven or Hell. Aquinas assured us that when the Messiah returns all the truths of Christianity will be scientifically true. But that day is not with us yet, and projecting the truth into an unknown future or a distant heaven doesn't of course make it any more true, but it does make any statements about the truth impossible to falsify.

The same problem holds true for those opinions individuals, groups or governments deem to be false. There is no way of demonstrating that either. No tests, no demonstrable proofs have ever been available which would convince those who are supposedly in error that their views are in fact false or wrong. Thus censorship of those opinions and beliefs which some find objectionable or offensive has been the method of choice for those who view persons who disagree with them to be infected with ideas that are false and vicious.

But if the censors mistake their opinions for the truth, their opponents are often no less guilty of the same mistake: In "the wars of Truth," Milton wrote, "Truth is strong . . . . And though all the windes of doctrin were let loose to play upon the earth, so Truth be in the field, we do injuriously by licencing and prohibiting to misdoubt her strength. Let her and Falsehood grapple; who ever knew Truth put to the wors, in a free and open encounter. Her confuting is the best and surest suppressing." (*Areopagetica*). This contention soon became the cornerstone of opposition to censorship in the modern world. In *An Apology for Printers*, Benjamin Franklin contended that "when Truth and Error have fair Play, the former is always an overmatch for the latter." Jefferson remarked in his First Inaugural Address, "[E]rror of opinion may be tolerated, when reason is left free to combat it" (Dumbauld 42-3); and the argument was central to the case against censorship in Mill's *On Liberty*.

The belief that truth is best served not by suppressing what one deems to be untrue but through the open, unfettered exchange of ideas is certainly correct, but it is correct only when it comes to questions of truth. That is why scientific study is made practically impossible in closed societies. But censorship has been undertaken in the name of Christianity for one because believers going all the way back to Paul understood quite correctly that open debate would not serve the furtherance of the faith, but would permit and even encourage differences of opinion. In the wars of truth open debate is the best, indeed the only method of establishing general consensus, but Milton, who acted as a government censor and even in his *Areopagetica* did not call for the lifting of prior restraints against popish doctrines, was focusing on wars not between competing truths, but between Catholic and Protestant beliefs, and no amount of free and open debate in the over three hundred years since Milton wrote has ever been able to resolve these difference and discover where the so-called truth lies. Harold Nelson has remarked that Milton's contention that truth will win out if allowed to grapple freely with falsehood has been questioned in recent years "because truth does not seem to emerge from a controversy in the automatic way [his] logic would lead us to expect" (32). The reason for that is simple. There is nothing wrong with Milton's logic. The problem is that truth can never emerge from a debate where the subject is not truth, and religious and moral differences, their claims to the contrary, do not involve issues that can be resolved in terms of truth or falsehood. Beliefs, opinions, moral and religious values cannot be shown to be either true or false. Just about every censor from Plato, to Augustine, to Lord Devlin has in one way or another recognized this fact. The use of censorship is itself an admission that one is not dealing with matters of truth and reason, since one after all does not need to enforce whatever can reasonably be demonstrated to be true nor repress whatever can be shown to be false! The Inquisition did not threaten to torture Galileo because it knew its view was the correct one. It threatened him with torture because it knew of no way of demonstrating to him that its doctrines were in fact the correct ones.

The same of course holds equally true for political opinions, for the "self-evident truths" Jefferson, for example, listed in *The Declaration of Independence*: most people, like let's say King George III, never took as self-evident, God-given truths that all men are endowed with the inalienable rights Jefferson enumerated. They were "true" because one particular group of men decided to publicize their opinions as truths; they were "true" for no other reason than that, as Jefferson declared, "*We hold* these truths to be self-evident."

Having said this, let me be clear about two points. The first is that free and open debate while it might not usually resolve differences of opinion is nevertheless a valuable thing when it comes to differences of opinion simply because it disallows the use of force as a method for achieving agreement. The great value of open debate within democracies is not that they will help us all better to discover just where the true opinion is to be found. The great value of democratic discourse is that it provides a framework for managing differences of opinion without the use of force. The great evil of censorship is not that it hides the truth or prevents men from arriving at it. In some cases it does indeed do just that. Rather the great evil of censorship is that it justifies the use of force as a legitimate means for dealing with differences of opinion!

Secondly, even though moral pronouncements cannot be shown to be either true or false, the reasons given to support them often can. It is neither a great truth nor a vicious falsehood that the races in America ought not to be segregated. But if one says that they ought to be integrated because integration fosters better understanding and tolerance or that they ought to be segregated because black people are inherently inferior to whites, the reasons given in each case amount to statements that can be tested and shown to be either true or not.

In *Crime and Punishment*, Dostoyevsky has his protagonist Raskolnikov note a remarkable fact that throughout history "the benefactors and arbiters of mankind have all shed rivers of blood." And Raskolnikov allows that Newton would have had the right to kill if such killing would help to further his ideas. However what Raskolnikov (and no doubt Dostoyevsky) did not understand is not simply that Newton did not murder, but that he did not have to. Jefferson would seem to have understood the situation better. He noted that "[m]illions of innocent men, women, and children, since the introduction of Christianity, have been burnt, tortured, fined, imprisoned [to produce uniformity of opinion]; and yet we have not advanced one inch toward uniformity." He recalled how the Inquisition reacted to Galileo's theories and compared that with the response Newton's received:

the Newtonian principle is now more firmly established, on the basis of reason, than it would be were the government to step in, and to make it an article of necessary faith. Reason and experiment have been indulged, and error has fled before them. . . . It is error alone [which] needs the support of government. Truth can stand by itself. (153)

Truth can indeed stand by itself, but it is not quite correct to say that it is error which needs the support of government because it is not the opposite of truth which governments enforce. Error can after all be refuted just as truth can be demonstrated. What needs the support of government is that which can neither be demonstrated nor refuted, that is, belief and opinion. What Jefferson seems not to have understood is that Newton succeeded where Christianity failed not simply or even primarily because he, as compared to Galileo, worked in a more enlightened country on the verge of a more enlightened age. Newton did not have to coerce, or censor or kill for his ideas as Protestants, Catholics, or Leninists have had to because he could demonstrate the truth of his ideas and they could not. As Newton himself noted in the preface to his *Opticks* the "design in this book is not to explain the properties of light by hypothesis, but to propose and *prove them by reason and experiments* . . ." (my italics).

One of the bases of censorship, as we have seen throughout, is the belief that the thoughts that men have are not simply different, but can be rated, ranked, and judged according to a hierarchy of values which would place men by virtue of what they think and feel and believe into superior and inferior positions. Whether men respond positively or negatively to certain types of expression, whether they assent to or dissent from the supposed truth of them or are stimulated or repulsed, aroused or offended by its content, becomes the test, the measure of whether individuals and groups of individuals posses superior gifts and powers or are ignorant and corrupt and need to be controlled. From this belief in the natural or irremediable inferiority of certain people, it follows that certain or most people can never be reasonably persuaded as to what is true and false, right and wrong, and their acceptance or conformity can only be gained through force or the fear of force. Much of this type of thinking would never have occurred and the kind of tyranny and oppression which follows from it might also not have occurred did men not, with what presumptuousness and arrogance, mistake their personal views for universal truth and presume as a consequence that those who disagreed were disagreeing with the truth and must therefore be ignorant, or mentally deficient, or corrupt, or depraved, or sinful, and that they who thought themselves in touch with the truth therefore had the right and the duty to enforce their views upon everyone else.

True heroism, Nietzsche said, is *not* fighting for what you believe in; but few men have ever been honored for such heroism. And when it comes to the blood that has been shed, the remarkable fact of human history is that the amount spilled by so-called mass murderers or serial killers like Jack the Ripper or the Boston Strangler is a spit in the ocean compared to those men who have fought for what they believed in simply because they could not possibly prove to others that they were right.

WORKS CITED

Alpert, Leo M. "Judicial Censorship of Obscene Literature." *Harvard Law Review* 52 (1938), 40-76.

Arcand, Bernard. *The Jaguar and the Anteater.* New York: Verso, 1993.

Arendt, Hannah. "Truth and Politics." *Between Past and Future.* New York: Viking Press, 1969.

Attorney General's Commission on Pornography: Final Report. Washington: GPO, 1986.

Augustine. *Political Writings.* Chicago: Regnery Press, 1962.

Blume, E. Sue. *Secret Survivors.* New York: John Wiley & Sons, 1990.

Broun, Heywood and Margaret Leech. *Anthony Comstock.* New York: Albert & Charles Boni, Inc., 1927.

Cassirer, Ernst. *Language and Myth.* New York: Dover Publications, 1953.

Causton, Bernard & G. Gordon Young. *Keeping It Dark.* London: Mandrake Press, n.d.

Choldin, Marianna Tax. *A Fence Around the Empire.* Durham: Duke University Press, 1985.

Christie Davies, "How our Rulers Argue about Censorship," *Censorship and Obscenity.* Eds. Rajeev Dhavan & Christie Davies. Totowa, New Jersey: Rowman and Littlefield, 1978.

Comstock, Anthony. *Frauds Exposed.* New York: J. H. Brown, 1880.
_____. *Traps for the Young.* Cambridge, Mass.: Harvard University Press, 1967.

Darnton, Robert. *The Forbidden Best-Sellers of Pre-Revolutionary France.* New York: W. W. Norton & Co., 1995.

Devlin, Patrick. *The Enforcement of Morals.* New York: Oxford University Press, 1972.

Dickey, Julienne. "Snakes and Ladders." *Feminism and Censorship.* Bridport, Dorset, England: Prism Press, 1988.

Dickey, Julienne & Gail Chester. "Introduction" *Feminism and Censorship.*

Diogenes Laertes. *Lives of Eminent Philosophers.* New York: G.P. Putnam's Sons, 1925.

Dumbauld, Edward, ed. *The Political Writings of Thomas Jefferson.* New York: The Bobbs-Merrrill Co., 1982.

Estes, James M. tr. *Whether Secular Government Has the Right to Wield the Sword in Matters of Faith: A Controversy in Nurenberg, 1530..* Toronto: Centre for Reformation and Renaissance Studies, 1994.

Farrington, Benjamin. *Greek Science.* Baltimore: Penguin Books, 1961.

Ferguson, William Scott. *Hellenistic Athens*. New York: Howard Fertug, 1969.

Garry, Ann. "Pornography and Respect for Women." *Pornography and Censorship*. Ed. David   Copp and Susan Wendell. Buffalo: Prometheus Books, 1983.

Gaur, Albertine. *A History of Writing*. New York: Cross River Press, 1992.

Gazzaniga, Michael S. *Nature's Mind*. New York: Basic Books, 1992

Graham, A.C., tr. *Chuang-tzu*. London: George Allen & Unwin, 1981.

Hamill, Pete. "Women on the Verge of a Legal Breakdown." *Playboy. 40* (January, 1993), 138+.

Henry, Alice. "Does Viewing Pornography Lead Men to Rape?" *Feminism and Censorship*.

Hippocratic Writings. Ed. G.E.R. Lloyd. New York: Penguin Books, 1978.

Hunt, Lynn. "Introduction." *The Invention of Pornography*. Ed. Lynn Hunt. New York: Zone Books, 1993.

Jacob, Francois. *The Logic of Life*. New York: Pantheon Books, 1982.

Jefferson, Thomas. *Notes on the State of Virginia*. New York: Harper & Row, 1964.

Itzin, Catherine. "Sex and Censorship." *Feminism and Censorship*.

Kendrick, Walter. *The Secret Museum*. New York: Viking Penguin, Inc., 1987.

Kon, Igor S. *The Sexual Revolution in Russia*. New York: The Free Press, 1995.

Lever, Maruice. *Sade*. New York: Farrar, Strauss, Giroux, 1993.

Levy, Leonard W. *Blasphemy*. New York: Alfred A. Knopf, 1993.

Lloyd, G.E.R. *Greek Science After Aristotle*. New York: W.W. Norton & Co., 1973.

Lockearht Commissionon Obscenity and Pornography, *Report*. Washington: GPO, 1970.

MacKinnon, Catherine. *Feminism Unmodified*. Cambridge: Harvard University Press, 1987.

_____. *Only Words*. Cambridge, Mass.: Harvard University Press, 1993.

Mandlestam, Nadezhda. *Hope Against Hope*. New York: Atheneum, 1976.

Mao Tse-tung. "On Democratic Centralism." *Chairman Mao Talks to the People*. New York: Pantheon Books, 1974

Mather, Cotton. *Cotton Mather on Witchcraft*. New York: Dorset Press, 1991.

McElroy, Wendy. *XXX: A Woman's Right to Pornography*. St. Martin's Press: New York, 1995.

Merck, Mandy. "Television and Censorship." *Feminism and Censorship.*

Money, John. "Paraphilias: Phenomenoly and Classification." *Venuses Penuses.* Buffalo: Prometheus Books, 1986.

Mura, David. "A Male Grief: Notes on Pornography and Addiction." *Men Confront Pornography.* New York: Crown Publishers, 1990.

Nelson, Harold L. *Freedom of the Press from Hamilton to the Warren Court.* Indianapolis: The Bobbs-Merill Co., 1967.

Oboler, Eli M. *The Fear of the Word.* Metuchen, N.J.: The Scarecrow Press, 1974.

Pagels, Heinz R. *The Dreams of Reason.* New York: Bantam Books, 1989.

Piaget, Jean. *Insights and Illusions of Philosophy.* New York: World Publishing Co., 1971.

Plato. *Phaedrus.* Cambridge: Cambridge University Press, 1952.

_____. *Protagoras.* York: Penguin Books, 1985.

_____. *The Seventh and Eigth Letters.* Harmondsworth: Penguin Books, 1977.

_____. *Timeus.* Baltimore: PenguinBooks, 1965.

Plutarch. *The Lives of the Noble Grecians and Romans.* New York: The Modern Library, n.d.

Popper, Karl. *Conjectures and Refutations.* New York: Harper & Row, 1968.

Putnam, George Haven. *The Censorship of the Church of Rome.* 2 vols. New York: Benjamin   Blom, 1967 (reissued from 1906).

Rembar, Charles. *The End of Obscenity.* New York: Simon & Shuster, 1970.

Report of the Arts Council of Great Britain on the Obscene Publications Act. In *The Obscenity Report.* London: Olympia Press, 1971.

The Report of the Commision on Obscenity and Pornography. New York: Bantam Books, 1970.

Robertson, Geoffrey. *Freedom, The Individual and the Law.* London: Penguin Boooks, 1991.

Romano, Carlin. "Between the Motion and the Act." *The Nation.* 257 (Nov. 15, 1993) 563-69.

St. John-Stevas, Norman. *Obscenity and the Law.* New York: Da Capo Press, 1974.

Schwartz, Louis B. "Morals Offenses and the Model Penal Code." *Morality and the Law.* Ed. Richard A. Wasserstrom. Belmont, Calif.: Wadsworth Publ. Co., 1971.

Sontag, Susan. "The Pornographic Imagination." *Styles of Radical Will.* New York: Anchor Books, 1996.

Sources of Chinese Tradition. Ed. William Theodore de Bary. New York: Columbia University Press

Starkey, Marion L. *The Devil in Massachusetts.* Time-Life Books: Alexandria, Va.: 1982.

Steiner, Wendy. *The Scandal of Pleasure.* The University of Chicago Press: Chicago, 1996.

Thompson, Bill. *Soft Core.* New York: Cassell, 1994.

Vance, Carole. "The Meese Commission on the Road." *Feminism and Censorship.*

Wallace, Jonathan & Mark Mangan. *Sex, Laws, and Cyberspace.* New York: Henry Holt & Co., 1996.

Wertham, Frederic. *Seduction of the Innocent.* Port Washington: N.Y.: Kennikat Press, 1972.

Widmer, Kinglsey & Eleanor, eds. *Literary Censorship,* Belmont, Cal.: Wadsworth Publishing, 1961.

Williams, Bernard, ed. *Obscenity and Film Censorship,* Cambridge: Cambridge University Press, 1981.

Williams, L. Pearce, ed. *Relativity Theory.* New York: John Wiley & Sons, 1968.

Williams, Roger. *The Bloudy Tenet. The Complete Writings of Roger Williams.* New York: Russell & Russell, Inc., 1963.

Winer, Joel H. *The War of the Unstamped.* Ithaca: Cornell University Press, 1969.

Zerubavel, Eviatar. *The Fine Line.* Chicago: University of Chicago Press, 1993.

Index